David & Charles
Newton Abbot London
North Pomfret (Vt) Vancouver

FOR MY PARENTS

British Library Cataloguing in Publication Data

Hanson, Harry
   Canal people.
    1. Canals – England – History 2. Labor
  and laboring classes – England 3. England
  – Social life and customs
  I. Title
  942   HE435

  ISBN 0–7153–7559–8

© Harry Hanson 1978

Set in Bembo (Series 270)
by HBM Typesetting Limited
Standish Street Chorley Lancashire
Printed in Great Britain
by Redwood Burn Limited Trowbridge
for David & Charles (Publishers) Limited
Brunel House Newton Abbot Devon

Published in the United States of America
by David & Charles Inc
North Pomfret Vermont 05053 USA

Published in Canada
by Douglas David & Charles Limited
1875 Welch Street North Vancouver BC

Contents

Acknowledgements

Thanks are due not only to librarians, curators and archivists in institutions throughout the country who assisted me in finding material, but also to those who humped weighty tomes around on my behalf, not least those at the Newspaper Library, Colindale. The House of Lords Record Office remains my favourite research institution and I again thank the staff who make visits there such a pleasure. I would also like to single out the Director and staff of the NSPCC headquarters, London; Mr A. Hayman, manager of the Bridgewater Department of the Manchester Ship Canal Co; Richard Hutchings, curator, British Waterways Museum, Stoke Bruerne, and Sheila Doeg of *Waterways News* (BWB Magazine), along with others who gave me permission to reproduce copyright material. Some copyright holders I have been unable to trace. To them I offer both thanks and apologies.

Edward Paget-Tomlinson supplied Plates 5, 9, 13, 14 and 26. Figs 2, 3, 5, 7, 9 and 11 are taken from *Illustrated Sporting and Dramatic News*, 13 May 1884 and Fig 6 from *Illustrated London News*, 10 October 1874, all reproduced by courtesy of the British Library. Mrs J. V. Greenhowe drew Figs 4, 8 and 15. Fig 12 was taken from *Bridgen's Directory of Wolverhampton*, 1833. The cartographer was Vic Welch.

Other individuals who assisted me were Paul Cope; Alan Harding; John Hemelryk; Jack Greenslade; Trevor King; Peter Norton; Cissie Purvis; Dr J. S. Taylor; Michael Ware. My sister, Vera Haydock, typed the manuscript. A word of thanks to my wife who sustained and encouraged me.

I am particularly grateful to David Campbell who loaned me his collection of newspaper cuttings and canal material. Mary Prior generously supplied me with many new sources. Professor A. E. Musson of Manchester University read through the manuscript, and made valuable suggestions and criticisms. My greatest debt is to Charles Hadfield who generously put his collection of canal material at my disposal, read the manuscript and suggested amendments.

Preface

Canal People sets out to describe the lives and labours of the men and women (and children) who worked upon the waterways of England and Wales from about 1760 to the virtual end of commercial carrying in the 1970s. It begins with those roisterous individuals who 'improved' rivers and dug out canals—the 'navigators'. It continues with the story of the watermen who followed in their wake—flatmen, keelmen, bargemen and boatmen—as well as with that of the men who ensured the passage of the vessels—maintenance men, lock-keepers, clerks, *et al*. 'Working' men are the heroes (and villains) of the narrative though one chapter does look at the 'guv'nors'. Comparisons with the watermen of other nations, particularly those of the USA, reveal that boat folk everywhere had much in common—and always they were a race apart.

The book is really a chronicle of the stories and adventures of waterway folk over two centuries. The approach is topical rather than strictly chronological, although there is a shift of emphasis from early to later years (and from faults to virtues) as the book progresses. There are pitfalls in jumping backwards and forwards across the centuries and it could appear that conditions remained much the same over 200 years. This was, of course, not so, although there were indeed some aspects of waterway life that changed relatively little. Similarly the selection and grouping together of events and misdemeanors of a like nature can give a misleading impression. For every person who gets his activities detailed in newspapers there are hundreds who do not. One hopes that in the book as a whole a balance is achieved which presents a rounded and honest picture of the people of the waterways.

The story begins with the importance of an expanding waterway system for the labouring population in the eighteenth century and examines the types of men who found employment there with all their faults and foibles. Women followed their husbands on to the vessels relatively early on and the peculiarities of this hardy breed are examined. Waterway work was tough indeed. We study the nature of the work with all its hardships and dangers especially as suffered by the children. Seen as Ishmaelites the boat people could expect little sympathy from landed society. We see how they helped each other through adversity until, belatedly, others began to concern themselves with the peculiar difficulties of waterway life. Briefly we focus upon one special breed of waterman—the owner boatman—and in particular upon one family—the Kings. In voyaging with these strange simple people through the trials and hazards (and compensations) of their calling the distinctive character, language and customs emerge to be documented in the penultimate chapter. Finally, sadly in some ways, but not in others, we see the canal people disappear.

Note: Decimal equivalents have not been given. Before 1971 there were 12 pennies (d) in 1 shilling (s) and 20 shillings in £1. One shilling = 5 new pence (p).

Introduction

To Lord Chatham the monarchy was a wonder. 'The least peep into the king's closet', said Edmund Burke, 'intoxicates him and will to the end of his life.' The pomp and pageantry of the Crown are a far cry from the simple intimacy of the English waterways, but, like Chatham with the King, those who venture into the canal world find an enchantment there which captures their minds and hearts.

Canals can mean many things to many men. Their 'pure placidity' provides an increasingly popular escape from the discords of modern living. There is the freedom of gypsy life in cruising to, and through, unknown, forgotten places, who knows exactly where—round Thrupp Bend, through Thrupp Wide and Thrupp; past Wychnor, Swarkestone and Merrybower, Marston Jebbett and Marston Doles; up or down Hoo Mill Lock, Nechells Shallow Lock and Gallows Inn Lock, not to mention Long Itchington Bottom Lock and Rumps Lock; over the Pontcysyllte Aqueduct; along Shebdon Embankment; through Curdley Tunnel and Tyrley Cutting; under Bakers Lane Turnover Bridge and Hurleston Roving Bridge, Miss Each Bridge and Catherine de Barnes Bridge, Redripes Bridge and Dirty Lane Bridge.

The simplicity of a canal bridge, the surge of water at a lock, the colourful roses and castles on a moving narrow boat have their own aesthetic attraction. The charm of the waterways lies in such things and much besides, but the most exhaustive guide book could not fully explain that intangible appeal which is just . . . canals.

Walter Bagehot, the great British constitutionalist, explained why the noble and imperious Chatham held a fellow mortal in such unlikely awe. He also made clear why the monarchy

Plate 1 The (new) Grand Union Canal at Watford—'the simplicity of a canal bridge' (*M. E. Ware*)

survived so successfully. 'Its mystery', he wrote, 'is its life.'

And it is perhaps the mystery of the canals that gives them their greatest appeal. The secrets of each leafy curve unfold to reveal yet another lying invitingly ahead. To voyage on the waterways is not to arrive.

More than that we journey into the mystery that was yesterday as we 'step with the utmost simplicity into the past'. For there are few glass-cased exhibits here to tell the whole story, only half glimpses of the past. The realities of locks and bridges, wharfs and warehouses, towpaths that have twisted down through time, are there at every turn on the 'cut', but the people are gone. Bricks and mortar and beaten earth can only hint at the hundred tales of flesh and blood in days long gone—tales of joy and sadness, as important in the lives of those people as in that of any king.

Follow the Trent & Mersey Canal through Rugeley. Benjamin Dykes, one of Pickfords' boatmen, abruptly lost his life there, when, according to the *Doncaster Gazette* of 17 February 1813:

As he was driving his horse . . . it became unruly and the rope by which he drew the boat unfortunately broke, and striking against the boatman was twirled by the force of the jerk several times round his body; in this situation the poor fellow was dragged by the horse sometimes in the canal, and sometimes on the towing path, till the rope at length broke, and left him in the water where he was found dead in a short time afterwards.

Twenty-six years later, at a spot a little further along the same canal, at the elbow-like bend known as Brindley's Bank, there was another tragedy. Here was found the bruised and violated corpse of Christina Collins.

It is exactly because they were the dramas of ordinary men and women that they have left little trace, and because the questions we ask are so difficult to answer we are the more intrigued. Where did they come from, those folk who once played such a vital role in the movement of England's goods? What kind of people were they—rich men, poor men, beggarmen, thieves? And where have they all gone?

'We must not', Bagehot cautions, 'let in daylight upon magic.' Perhaps we might 'peep into the closet'.

Plate 2 The Llangollen Canal near Chirk—'The secrets of each leafy curve unfold to reveal yet another lying invitingly ahead. To voyage on the waterways is not to arrive' (*Author*)

I

New Opportunities

From the time that the hunter became a farmer down into the eighteenth century, most British men (and women) were born to work upon the land. The good earth itself is the greatest and often the only memorial to the labours of those untold millions who have enriched the soil in the service of man. Individually they have left little trace. Scrawled entries in musty parish registers briefly record the comings and goings of some, but for many an unmarked grave hides where the land took back its own. Occasionally, further scanty details of their life and work enable us to draw out a few individuals from the anonymous multitude.

Thomas Fogg was one of those who brushed lightly across history's canvas—as a farm labourer at Barnton in Cheshire. He was poor, being often at the mercy of the Poor Law authorities for survival. He was unlucky too. In 1770 his wife died, leaving him with several young children to care for. There was nothing particularly unusual about the experiences of this obscure northern labourer. Poverty and tragedy in one form or another were the lot of many an agricultural worker in eighteenth-century Britain.

Thomas had a son, William, whose birth in 1763 came perhaps more as a burden than a blessing. For the son, in turn, it was hardly an auspicious start to life to be born and reared in poverty; motherless from the age of seven, with every prospect of his father's life being relived in his own. William may well have set out upon the same path, for he probably followed his father onto the land. The significance of William Fogg lies not in his farming life, but in the fact that he left it—in company with many others.[1]

Through Barnton flows the river Weaver, first made navigable by an Act of 1721 and much improved by a further Act of 1760. Demands for Cheshire salt increased and with them demands for 'flats' and 'flatmen' to carry it down the river.

William Fogg was tempted aboard one of these sailing vessels and he never looked back. By 1795 he had risen to be master of Jonadab Mort's flat, *Ann*, taking salt from his Northwich works down to Liverpool for export, returning with coal loaded on the Sankey Navigation.[2] Had he followed in the steps of his father he might have come to earn perhaps 10s a week. As the captain of a flat his 'emoluments' would be at least £80 per annum.

Paradoxically, although it was the advance of the powered machine which brought rapid and remarkable changes—the Industrial Revolution—to a largely rural Britain in the period 1760–1830, for many crucial years it was the age-old forces of wind and tide and the muscles of man and horse which maintained and even increased the momentum of change through the cheap transportation of bulky commodities vital to industrial development—coal, iron ore and iron, cotton, salt, clay, limestone, manure, agricultural produce and building materials. Inland navigation was a 'growth' industry and despite its ancient antecedents it was, in many ways, a new one. Thousands of men who took to the water were to rise from being penniless slaves of the land to be masters of vessels, owning an independence and wealth unthought of when they and their fathers toiled at the drudgery of tilling the soil.

There were other 'growth' industries too, of course. Labouring men seized similar opportunities in the cotton, iron, coal, engineering, pottery and other industries. The experiences of such men give the lie to much that has been written of this period in British history—one which has insinuated its miseries into the subconscious of the average citizen like no other in British history.

There is no denying that these were difficult years. As the first industrial nation Britain could not look elsewhere for guidance. She was also, at a crucial time (1793–1815), caught up in a long and costly military struggle with her oldest enemy, France. This made change all the more rapid and adaptation to it all the more painful. In particular, the capital which might have been used for social amelioration was sucked in to create the forces of destruction necessary for the defeat of Napoleon.

None the less, as more success stories like those of William Fogg are brought to light, it is becoming clear that there was as much (and probably more) progress as poverty during the Industrial Revolution and that the miseries which have made such compulsive reading have been overdone. (Not least have the supposed hardships endured through the rapid enclosure of land and the spread of the power loom been greatly exaggerated.[3]) For many, and probably most, in the generation that worked through the turn of the century, the dramatic changes brought opportunities which often gave a status and prosperity to working men undreamed of a few decades before. New occupations appeared and growing demands brought a greater dimension to the old—not elast on the waterways.

Peter French was another Barnton man. Born in 1730, the son of a farm labourer, he followed his father onto the land. In 1775, French, like Fogg, was tempted to seek his fortune on the river as a flatman. It was in that same year that navvies by the score descended upon Barnton to cut the Trent & Mersey Canal and later he forsook the river for boating on the new waterway. He too did well for himself. By 1795 he was the master of a canal barge taking John Gilbert's salt down from Marston to Runcorn.[4] We can be sure that he earned far more than a farm labourer, though less than if he had stayed among the flats and been made a master like William Fogg.

One of the labourers who came to Barnton to finish the canal in 1776 was John Proctor. Of him we know little beyond the fact that from 1770 he worked a year on the farm of James Winder at Elland in Yorkshire for which he was paid six guineas (and probably board and lodging). He then worked as a day labourer for John MacKay Esq in Lancashire, presumably as a farmhand, but soon left to work as a navvy on the Chester Canal from whence he moved to the Trent & Mersey. By 1795 a John Proctor was master of one of William Davies' canal boats working between Tipton and Fazeley, earning far in advance of the sum John Proctor, farm labourer, would ever have done.[5]

New opportunities were not restricted to those who built the canals or navigated vessels upon them. There were jobs too for agents, wharfingers, warehousemen, clerks, porters, toll-collectors, lock-keepers, carpenters, masons, bricklayers, lengthsmen and labourers. They were attracted by good wages and opportunities for advancement as well as by the greater job security. For if a lock-keeper or even a labourer did his duty, he was guaranteed a steady job and income for the rest of his life. And there were perks—usually a house with a fair-sized garden, rent free, along with the coal to heat it. On retirement most were granted a pension or gratuity.

The concept of 'inland navigation' was not a phenomenon of the Industrial Revolution. The main British rivers had long been used to carry goods; the advantage of water transport being well understood. This was simply that many more goods could be moved by water than over land using the same motive power. One horse could pull less than one ton over hilly and muddy roads; by water he could pull as much as 60 tons, when river conditions were at their best, the current slight and the water deep. Rivers that were naturally navigable were rarely so obliging, being prone to drought and flood, and even in their everyday state they often fell below the optimum for navigation. On the Thames, even under normal conditions, five, six and more horses (or twice and even three times as many men) were needed to pull the heavily laden 'western barges' up through the stiff current.

In the century after the restoration of Charles II the limits of navigation were edged upstream. 'Navigations' began to appear. That is, the rapid, twisting, shallow waters of rivers like the Irwell, Weaver, Douglas, Aire and Calder were slowed, deepened and straightened to make them navigable, using the pound lock. It was then but a short step to the creation of artificial waterways, levelled and still—canals—in new areas, thus taking the advantages of water transport into the very heart of the country.

With hindsight we can see that there was nothing really revolutionary about the improvements and changes to the inland navigation system in the eighteenth century. It is simply the story of man's increasing ability to extend and yet tame to his (almost) absolute obedience the mighty and destructive force that water can be—the Duke of Bridgewater was wont to call water 'the best of friends and the worst of enemies'. This activity was in response to growing demands for improved transportation. The results, in conjunction with many other important factors, *were* to be revolutionary. For the consequent reduction in the price of bulky goods was to have a tremendous impact upon the development of the economy as 'the greatest burdens of the commercial world . . . [came to be] borne steadily, silently and without visible sign of their extent, like woes in some human lives . . .'.[6]

The real breakthrough came with the first inland canal which resulted from the enterprise of the eccentric Duke of Bridgewater and his two able assistants, John Gilbert, his capable agent, and James Brindley, his semi-literate engineer. It was the success of their short canal, which from about 1761 reduced the price of the Duke's Worsley coal by half in Manchester, which was to 'diffuse a spirit of navigation through the very heart of the kingdom'. It was a 'diffusion' which followed very much at the heels of Brindley who was in great demand to engineer the canals which followed. He was seen as 'a little man upon a muddy horse, for ever tired and for ever riding', as he attempted to oversee the foundation of the canal system almost single handed. Worn out by his exertions and his diabetes he lived to see very little of it completed.

It was not in the north west of England, however, that canals were to have their greatest immediate impact, but in the Midland counties where a dearth of navigable rivers and bad roads meant that the means of transportation were inadequate for the growing demands of the metal industries. The Duke of Bridgewater did go on to extend his canal to the Mersey estuary at Runcorn by 1776 and a mighty work it was, but as early as 1772 Birmingham had been connected by canal with the coalfields at Wednesbury (1769) to the north west, with the river Severn at Stourport in the west, the river Trent in the east and with Stone in Staffordshire in the north. Long before the Duke's more famous waterway was complete the groundwork of the Midland canal system had been laid.

Canals were very much a Midland phenomenon. From here the network expanded. Here were the real opportunities for men to take up a completely new and profitable way of life. Already by January 1769 there were 1,000 navvies at work on the Staffordshire & Worcestershire and Trent & Mersey Canals, together with a further 500 and more on the Birmingham. Construction was also under way on the Coventry and Oxford Canals.

Work began with local men, but there were not enough. Skilled craftsmen in particular were soon at a premium. It was not long before the agents of each canal company were out

scouring the countryside for more labour. The Duke of Bridgewater had to look to Yorkshire for masons in 1767 and for
labourers in 1772.[7] Some were not above poaching men from
other companies. The Staffordshire & Worcestershire Canal
Company suspected foul play in 1767 when a large number of
men slipped away from the works, among them 'Johnathan
Melloday of a brown complexion and squints with an eye and is
about 5ft 5in'. There was a stern warning for anyone employing
him or his fellows. They could 'depend on being proceeded
against as the Law directs . . .'.[8] In the following year it was the
Birmingham Canal Company's turn. The Droitwich Navigation
Company had 'enticed away Stone cutters' from the works, the
minutes of 7 October recorded in disgust.

In July 1776 the Stroudwater Navigation Company ordered
Edmund Lingard to 'immediately set out for the North to treat
with some more Persons to come and undertake the cutting' and
by 9 August he had 'been to several places in Warwick and
Leicestershire . . . and engaged with a considerable number of
men . . .'.

Evidence like this contradicts suggestions that these men were
poorly paid. Clearly there was a shortage of canal labour, and
workers in short supply are usually well paid. Nor are men lured
away from works, or from Leicestershire to Stroud without
'good encouragement'. What else brought John Proctor from
Lancashire to Chester and Barnton, or men from Wales, Cornwall,
Somerset and Derbyshire to the Sapperton tunnel on the Thames
& Severn Canal?[9]

Canal labour was again in great demand in the 1790s and 1800s
with the second surge of canal construction. The net was cast far
and wide. Advertisements tempting 'Canal Cutters, Drainers and
Miners' to the Midland canal works shared the *Birmingham Gazette*
with similar notices from far away Lancashire companies. Down
in Exeter readers of the *Flying Post*, on 30 August 1810, learned
that there was a need for 'Two or Three Hundred Good Workmen
on the Worcester and Birmingham Canal' 150 miles to the north.
Handbills lured labourers out of the Welsh mountains to the
Monmouthshire Canal.

Of course, there was always an element of local labour in the
building of any canal. The bulk of the labouring work on the

Duke's canal was carried out by men 'in the district' and before 1770 almost exclusively so.[10] Part of the labour force on the Thames & Severn Canal, under construction in the mid 1780s, was drawn from the ranks of men unemployed because of a depression in the local clothing trade. On the Basingstoke Canal in the late 1780s preference was given to employing local labour at the request of the proprietors.

Most of these men, to the chagrin of the local farmers, would be agricultural workers. It was from the Basingstoke Canal that a sub-contractor absconded with the wages of his 'many country hands'.[11] One MP railed against the 'present ruinous rage' for canals, demanding that the 'persons who cut them' be restricted from employing labour in the harvest months.[12]

The years from 1793, however, were rather special. There was a war on. Men were syphoned off to the army and navy. The canal construction boom went on regardless. Dislocations to grain imports made harvests even more important than usual and the war had also been an important factor in the stimulation of Irish and Scottish agriculture. This kept at home many of the Irishmen and Scotsmen, who, along with the Welsh, had traditionally journeyed to England for the various harvests. No doubt some of these had become involved in canal-building too.

The Celts were not the only wanderers. Some English agricultural labourers were also surprisingly mobile. There were other men like John Proctor who might work for a farmer one year and in the next be with another many miles away. Men like this would think nothing of tramping 50 miles on hearing of well paid work in canal construction.

It has been suggested that it was the Enclosure Acts which impoverished these men and forced them to leave their home villages to live and labour in navvy encampments because their land and rights to land had been unfairly taken from them.

Now it is perfectly true that there was rural poverty over large areas of the south and east Midlands during the Industrial Revolution and this was where most enclosures took place, but the one did not generally stem from the other. Many were landless labourers before enclosures. If anything the parcelling up of land increased job opportunities for such men because of the need for more people to work at fencing, hedging, ditching and road-building and because a greatly increased acreage was brought under cultivation, growing more labour-intensive crops like the turnip and potato. It was simply that the population outgrew the job opportunities where—unlike in the north and north-west Midlands—there was no industry near enough to attract away the surplus. The tragedy in these pauper counties was that most people did not leave.

Some did. There are many reasons why a man leaves his childhood home. Sometimes they are discreditable and so they were then, but often it is the strong and the able, the men of initiative and enterprise, who are attracted away, leaving the timid, the halt and the poor to their misery.

Canal-builders were not interested in paupers, local or otherwise. 'Strong, able Men' were the people they were after. Sometimes it is true that proprietors were eager to employ the local poor because this reduced the poor rates they themselves were paying, but the engineers and contractors were not. As one might have complained in 1788 '. . . while these industrious poor are by all their efforts incapable of earning a sustenance, those who are brought from similar works, cheerfully obtain comfortable support'.[13]

Early on in the Canal Age contractors built up their own corps of elite workers who travelled with them from works to works. In 1768 the Birmingham Company advertised for 'several Foremen and Undertakers, who perfectly understand the Nature of Navigation Business, and can bring with them a sufficient number of Workmen . . .'.[14] Such bodies of men may well have existed before the Canal Age, working on river improvements and other public works. The Fenland 'bankers', long skilled in digging and draining, could have formed the nucleii of the early corps.

Though men were always joining and leaving the ranks of canal-builders, the number of permanent 'professionals' increased apace in the eighteenth century until there were legions of itinerant navigators moving singly or together from one canal works to another. Most were drawn from a life of labour on the land and it was the top end of that stratum, in physique and enterprise, if not necessarily in morals, which was creamed away. But there were all sorts and conditions of men at work on the waterways—men like John Catharall, 'of a dark complexion, Pockmark'd, and has been a drummer 5′ 7″' at work on the Staffordshire & Worcester Canal in 1766.[15]

If strong able 'bankers', 'cutters', 'diggers' and 'navigators' were, like skilled craftsmen, invariably in short supply, the situation was not improved by the propensity of the men to move about in hopes of better wages, which, occasioned 'much inconvenience and loss to people engaged in such Concerns'.

If such shortages meant higher wages, the navvies almost certainly earned them, for the work was often long, hard and dangerous. On the Calder & Hebble Navigation in 1761 it was ordered that 'the Men . . . shall not work more than 12 hours per Day unless in Cases of Emergency'. Canal company minutes often recorded how men had been 'much hurt and bruised in the Company's works' or 'lamed and rendered sick'.

Few details of how the 'hurts' and 'bruises' and worse were come by are given. The *Doncaster Gazette* of 10 June 1803 explains what could happen when

George Sharp, a canal contractor and three other men, employed in the tunnel of the Huddersfield Canal, near Marsden, having set what is technically called a blast, to blow up the fragments of rock, retired to witness the explosion. An unusual time having elapsed . . . they supposed it was extinguished and approached nearer, when the powder unhappily exploded, and killed George Sharp on the spot; two of his fellow workmen were dreadfully bruised, and remained blind for some time, and the others received several wounds from the splinters of the rock.

Tunnels claimed many victims. Two workmen on their way out to breakfast paused under a ventilation shaft on the Thames & Medway Canal in 1822. Just at that moment the roof caved in and engulfed them. Though rapidly dug out one of them was found 'quite dead and the other had one of his legs broken and much bruised'. Two years earlier another navvy working in one of the same shafts fell 130ft to his death and, in falling on two other men, seriously injured them as well.[16]

There were accidents enough out on the line of the canal too, like the one to Joseph Ainsley at work on a canal near Sheffield in

1815, when 'a large quantity of earth gave way and fell upon him' and he was 'dreadfully crushed'.[17]

Some companies cared for their injured men. James Whitworth, who hurt his hand in building the Rochdale Canal, was 'allowed 5s per Week towards his support till he became able to work again'.[18] The Manchester Bolton & Bury Company spent money 'in assisting poor persons who have been lamed and rendered sick in the Service of the Company and unfit to work ...'.[19] The Huddersfield contributed 5s a week to a sick club formed by the men working on the Standedge tunnel where deaths and injuries were appallingly frequent.[20] Other companies encouraged the men to pay into similar 'Sick and Hurt clubs'. They subscribed to the hospitals which tended their wounded workers. They often paid for a dead man to be buried. An agricultural labourer might have expected much less from his employers. And frequently the men were not, strictly speaking, employed by the companies, but by numerous contractors, large and small, who built the different sections of each canal.

Sharing danger and hardship in their life and work together; seen and feeling themselves as outcasts from society; often far from home, there grew up among these men a rough loyalty and comradeship which was most in evidence when they honoured their dead. When young Samuel Marshall died on the Ancholme Navigation works in 1826 his remains were

> ... borne to the church ... on the shoulders of six of his comrades, and the pall sustained by as many female friends. Upwards of 300 of his associates, each decorated with a white ribbon walked in procession, and the whole was preceeded by singers from the neighbourhood. The procession was conducted throughout with great order and silence ....

There were 800 navvy mourners in the cortège following the remains of another banker to his grave, a man drowned in the river Witham near Bardney in 1815. Every hat was decorated with a blue ribbon as a mark of respect for their comrade. Each man subscribed 2s 6d into a fund, part of which was 'expended in regaling themselves' after the funeral. The rest they gave to the bereaved widow.[21]

The villagers of Bardney were soon to see another side to these men who had marched to church with such humility. The building of a waterway in country districts often meant that there was little accommodation and provision for large numbers of men. 'The labourers for cutting the canal are much imposed upon by the extravigant Charges of the Innkeepers' a Leeds & Liverpool Canal committee man had noticed in January 1771. No doubt it was much the same in Bardney with the tradesmen milking the navvies for every penny they could. They and the villagers lived to regret it. A dispute with the baker grew into a full scale riot as enraged navvies tore pubs apart, drank all the beer 'on the house', robbed the villagers and fought the constables—one of whom died. Only the arrival of the cavalry saved the village from worse.[22]

The Leeds & Liverpool Company, once aware of the problem, rented accommodation and provided 'proper provisions' for their 'diggers' and so did other companies, but some did not, leaving the navvies at the mercy of unscrupulous suppliers.

Provisions were of vital importance to the men. Hard work demanded hard feeding and no doubt much of their earnings went in assuaging voracious appetites, an example of which is illustrated by the 'supper' eaten by twenty-five bankers working on the Dearne & Dove Canal in 1801. At the Red Lion Inn they ate and drank 40lb of beef, 36lb of potatoes, 20lb of pudding, 18lb of bread and a quantity of ale equal to 150lb weight, which amounted to $10\frac{1}{2}$lb each man.

Pay was another problem area. It was not that the men were inadequately paid. Rather, it often seemed to them that they would never be paid at all. At one meeting, on 12 January 1798, of the Stratford-upon-Avon Canal Company the proceedings were unusually animated when 'a great number of Labourers employed in the Canal attended . . . very Clamorous for the Money due to them and . . . in great distress for want of the same'. They were pacified with promises, but sometimes similar incidents got out of hand as when the men working on the Grand Western Canal, aggrieved at the delay in the payment of their wages, got drunk all over the area, committed 'various excesses' and finished up with a riot on the evening of Sampford Peverell cattle fair. Three hundred of them laid siege to the house of an unfortunate Mr Chave and the night ended in injury, death and destruction.[23]

Plate 3 Navvies collecting wages during the building of the Manchester Ship Canal in the early 1890s—descendants of the 'savage ungovernable banditti' (*Manchester Ship Canal Co*)

The common practice of paying the men by the month, and not always then, led to the storing up of wants which included giant thirsts. By the second phase of canal-building there were far more navvies who were 'strangers in the country' at each works. Such men were often uninhibited by family and community, 'owning no tie', working far from any effective forces of law and order.

Little wonder that, after a month or more of hard labour and abstinence, when the men *were* paid they made up for it. Sometimes a festering sense of collective grievance about the work, the pay, or the provisions was brought to a head by alcohol and one thing led to another. Navvies seemed often to be in the thick of some 'riotous affray', or were 'assembling' and 'parading' in a 'very riotous manner' following pay day (or because of the lack of it), which is no doubt why they were thought by some to be 'a constant nuisance to the neighbourhood and the terror of all descriptions of people', while others saw them as 'a savage ungovernable banditti'.

The navvies working on the Leicester & Northamptonshire Union became something of a nuisance in 1795. The business was sparked off by the arrest of two drunken navvies in a Kilworth shop. No doubt the authorities expected trouble, for when the drunkards were taken off to Leicester for trial they had an escort of forty soldiers—to no avail. The massed hordes of the navvies descended upon the 'Fencibles' and put them to rout, freeing their comrades in the process. When word reached Leicester the enraged military buzzed out to swarm over the countryside in search of the rioters, led by the Loyal Leicester Volunteer Infantry who, in their haste, forgot the ammunition. The Volunteer Cavalry thundered after them and within several days a goodly number of rioters were rounded up.[24]

Even if members of the local community did manage to escape 'turbulance and riot' at the hands of the navigators, it did seem to them that crime was on the increase when navvies were near. Had they not all read of the 'two men working at the . . . Canal . . . apprehended for sheep stealing?' They had all heard of 'John Ward, . . . making a disturbance at the White Lion, and demolishing a chair . . .', even if they had not been there themselves. The terrible assault by three canal navigators on 'a person near the Common Pond (back gate of Mrs Chivers)' where 'the man was kicked in the ribs until he became senseless', was a talking point for days.

It is too easy to select examples of criminal behaviour among the navvies and label them all as being dishonest, violent, brutal men, and much besides. There were some rugged characters amongst them, and some bad ones. But many miles of canal were built peaceably enough. Much depended on how the men were handled by the contractors, engineers and canal companies. No doubt many did their work, perhaps even saved what money they could for some dreamed-of venture of their own—a piece of land, a horse to go boating, even a boat—and troubled nobody. We need to find out much more about these men before we can judge them in the round.

It was probably not until the second wave of canal construction that the navvies came to have a distinctive identity as a separate sub-cultural group with customs peculiar to their occupational calling. The emergence of this sub-culture is really part of another story and one which continues into Terry Coleman's *Railway Navvies*, for many of the interesting traditions of the railway builders can be traced back into the Canal Age. The practice of using nicknames, for example, was common among the canal navvies.

A man's 'bye-name' often reflected his origins, like Yorkshire Jemmy or Yorkshire Billy—sometimes known as Slender Jane. There was Northamptonshire Tom who with Red Jack had 'terrorised every county they have resided in'.

Of an evening, when the hard day's work was done, the men would gather around an outdoor fire, in a smoke-filled hut or in some pub. One of their number would be pushed forward with much back slapping and raucous encouragement to do his turn—a ribald ditty accompanied by thunderous choruses. Another burly navvy would step forward to do a jig. They loved to dance. A plaintive ballad might follow amidst a hushed silence as they, the great unloved, thought of home and loved ones—perhaps lost loved ones.

It was at times like this that Fiddler Sam would come into his own. Tall, broad-shouldered, 'a remarkable clean made straight fellow', light-haired and heavily whiskered, he was 'well known amongst the Bankers from whistling and tuning to them whilst they are dancing'.

Thomas Lister, condemned and hung at Lincoln, was known to his comrades as Clainhim for reasons only they knew. Crooked Stockings had a price on his head for stealing a shotgun. Slender Dick, his real name of Richard Poucher long forgotten, had incongruously thin and rather bandy legs made to seem thinner through supporting unusually thick strong loins. He was distinctive too for his long face and large Roman nose turned up at the end and broken in the middle from constant fights. Timothy Brammer's favourite pursuit is clear, if not from his nose then from his nicknames, Tiger or Rough Tom, and so is Thomas Strong's, better known as Tippler or Old Tip. These three 'working Bankers or Navigators' had been 'pursued from one public work to another from one end of the kingdom to the other' in order to bring them to justice for an armed robbery at William Elsey's Hawstead Hall near Horncastle.

Drinking, violence and theft—were these three men typical of the canal navvying class at its apogee? Perhaps. If so, they certainly parted from this life in what was thought to be true navvy tradition 'fearing no law' for as the judge 'in a peculiarly affecting language and tone proceeded to pass the dreadful sentence of death upon them. . . , [the] prisoners bore it with considerable affrontery . . .', and on leaving the dock Tippler shouted, 'If I go to hell Old Elsey will go with me'.[25]

2
Some 'Bominable Bad Uns

A strong element of the likes of Tiger, Tippler and Slender Dick seems to have been passed on into the ranks of the canal boatmen, whose quarrelsome and violent nature, morals and drinking habits also became something of a by-word. In 1877 a newspaper reporter ventured into the unknown world of the English waterways conscious that:

> Bargees bear the reputation of being uncouth and semi-civilised folk very averse to the entertainment of strangers, as a class keeping much to themselves, and not freely communicative to the casual wayfarer of the city except in the way of foul-mouthed objurgation.

He was further discouraged at the outset by a long-serving canal-company official who cautioned him: 'There are some 'bominable bad uns among 'em. I believe some of 'em would as soon kill a man as look at him.' The journalist did indeed find that 'the bargee is not a person altogether after my own heart'.

The unfortunate facial appearance of navvies like Slender Dick, where life had not improved on nature's failure, seems to have been in evidence too, for the boatman had 'as a rule a stolid heavy ignorant look about him, which gives him the appearance of a man quite capable of committing any brutal assault without actually intending it. He might knock down his wife, for instance, and maim her, "all in fun" . . .'.[1]

A boatman like Charles Hodgkiss, forty-four years old, would have afforded the newspaper man a perfect example. Brought to court in 1832, he was described, in the uninhibited reporting of the time, as being 'an ill-favoured man having a broken nose . . .'. Appearing in the same case was his nineteen year old mate,

27

William Cook, whose appearance was also 'by no means in his favour'.

Hodgkiss seems to have developed a violent hatred for another boatman—the elderly Francis Wassell—whose body was dragged out of the Stourport basin. Whether Hodgkiss had put him there is not clear, but Joseph Longmore, a boatman, had earlier heard him mutter, 'I will be his butcher before the week is out'.

William Cook gave his account of what happened on the night of Wassell's death. On leaving The Bell at around half past ten 'Old Frank' asked Cook to go and sleep with him. Hodgkiss then stepped out of the pub yard and walked off with Wassell. He heard Hodgkiss ask Wassell if he would let *him* sleep on his boat.

Wassell hesitated.

'If you won't I'll mill you,' growled Hodgkiss.

'Go it then,' replied 'Old Frank', whereupon Hodgkiss struck the older man several times and 'jowled his head against the wall'.

When they got down to Wassell's boat Hodgkiss asked again if he could sleep on board, and on once more being refused he shouted, 'I will drown you; and I'll serve them the same that are with you, if you have anybody with you.'

Whereupon, according to Cook, he pushed 'Old Frank' into the canal.[2]

'Such quarrels are common with the boatmen,' a watchman told another court in Manchester after he had seen a similar fight on the Rochdale Canal, which had also ended in the death of a boatman. He did not interfere because 'had he meddled with them, the windows of the factory would probably have been broken'.

From inside his factory he saw James Hanson clamber from a barge on to the banks of the canal to gather up stones and slates.

'Damn thee, I'd cut thy bloody head off,' he shouted. 'If I could find a stone, I'd make thee remember throttling me.'

A man pushed his head through the hatchway of the boat and shouted back, 'Go away, go away. I'll have no more to do with thee.'

'Damn thee, I'll murder thee,' Hanson replied hurling stones and further angry insults at the man on the boat.

All eventually went quiet, but in the morning William Cheetham was found dead in his bunk, his head smashed in.[3]

Plate 4 The lock and temptations to passing boatmen at 'Kinfare' (Kinver) on the Staffordshire & Worcestershire Canal about 1906. Charles Hodgkiss lingered here too long in 1832 (*M. E. Ware*)

Drinking lay at the bottom of much of the 'bominableness of the watermen. Hodgkiss had begun drinking at 'Kinfare' five days before they reached Stourport. He became and remained so drunk that he later admitted, 'he did not know what day he came to Stourport' and there were further visits to The Bell on the night of Wassell's death.

In fact, Hodgkiss survived the accusations of murder—William Cook's evidence was considered unreliable—but seven years later his excesses again came to light when he was charged with being drunk in Liverpool Road, Stoke, and indecently exposing his person. In his defence he said that he had 'met with an old friend and taken a "drop too much"'.[4]

Hanson, in the second murder case, had been with Cheetham, and their captain, Clayton, to a public house in Manchester where, in the course of the evening, they all became 'far advanced in liquor'. They returned to the Brownlow Arms where the boat horses were stabled and drank some more. From there the drunken quarrel developed which was to end in tragedy.

It was at another pub—the Unicorn in Scale Lane, Hull—that a dispute between Thomas Riggs, master of a Wakefield sloop, and Thomas Parker, a keelman in the Knottingley trade, again turned violent. They agreed to adjourn to the quay to fight where 'after a quarter of an hour's contention Thomas Parker lost his life in the affray'.[5]

The flatmen of the early nineteenth century were, in their turn, considered to be 'a most drunken, dissolute and disorderly Body of men'.[6] Heavy drinking was widely recognised as being an evil of the canals. There was plenty of drunkenness on land too, but the boatmen often had a more ready access to a cheap supply—a free supply in fact—because large quantities of liquor were carried on the canals. One agent in the 1830s, disturbed by the late arrival of the fly-boat at Lancaster, decided to walk along the towpath in search of it. He found the boat lying across the canal; the horses grazing quietly on the bank. Getting on board he found the crew lying about helplessly drunk—'soaked with rum *inside* and *out*', from one of the hogsheads in the cargo.[7]

John Hollins, a clergyman who interested himself in the boatmen in the 1840s and 1850s, remarked sadly on the generality of drunkenness. One day, on putting a tract on *The Evils of Drunkenness* into the hands of a boatman, the recipient remarked soberly 'I helped to get a dead man out of the water last voyage who was drowned while drunk,' and Hollins added, 'Time after Time did I, from one and another, receive intelligence of boatmen drowned too often, alas, in a state of intoxication'.[8]

The evil continued. One boatman in 1898 admitted to spending £1 a week on average over several years on drink, and another in 1910 to having been on some tremendous benders.

Once when I was going to Staffordshire I spent all my 'starting money' at 'The Ship' and walked into the Severn while trying to get aboard the steam tug, was pulled out by the captain, kept all night in my wet clothes, and when found in the morning by my wife was penniless and very wretched. Another time I and three more watermen went with our boat from Birmingham to London. We drank and gambled all our money on the way up, and starved our horses that the corn money might follow the rest. We stayed at Stratford, and cooking up a tale to one of our employers, telegraphed for money and spent this in the same way, and had to be fetched home by our wives. After such doings you will not wonder that I ended by getting to prison.[9]

Later in this century, when the last of the fly–boats were still thrusting their way importantly through the night down the Shropshire Union Canal, sometimes the crews were 'well primed with "courage" before leaving Chester'.[10] And in the 1920s there was the woman bargee who, in passing through Leeds, very frequently 'slipped on banana skins'. At least that was the explanation she often gave as to how she received her frequent black eyes and other injuries. A missioner who knew her failing for strong drink, once asked jocularly, on seeing her in a particularly damaged condition, 'Another banana skin, mother?'

'Tek thi' 'ook,' replied the offended woman.[11]

Drink could be a problem with the canal staff too, at least for a part of the nineteenth century. In 1835 five labourers on maintenance work at the Eastwood Lock on the River Dun Navigation adjourned for several hours to the York Keel in Masborough where they had 10 quarts of ale among them. Back at work Thomas Ellis and John Lambert began a quarrel which escalated into dirt-throwing and finally Ellis threw 'a large piece of coal, which struck the deceased on the head with such force and violence that his cap was cut through and part of the skull driven into the brain'.[12]

Drunkenness reached higher levels than labourers. One night in 1830 all the men, including the agents, at Hargreaves' Preston warehouse had got so drunk that no one was in a fit state to take the loaded train of waggons up the tramway to Walton Summit where a boat waited to take the goods, mainly butter, to the Manchester market. Fear not, young Myles Pennington was there.

'Knowing its vast importance,' he related proudly, 'I harnessed up a team of horses and started on my night journey, and with the exception of a few mishaps, one of which was getting off the track and having to rouse up a neighboring [sic] farmer to help me on again, I reached Summit in safety and was received with three cheers by the boatmen.'

This sort of thing often stemmed from the practice of the agent taking samples from spirits in transit to make sure that they had not been interfered with. This caused bouts of drunkenness in offices and warehouses as well as starting many an agent on the downward path to alcoholism.

All sorts of people assisted at the loading of a boat—porters, clerks, the wharfinger and the boatmen themselves—all overseen by the captain, for faulty loading could lead to the capsizing of his craft. In filling the boat with heavy, bulky goods like coal and salt there were special loaders employed to speed the process. It became the custom for the captain to pay the loaders himself for help in trimming the cargo—a perk known as 't'lowance'. This was usually spent on beer which was consumed in vast quantities. One observer, as a young boy on an errand in a pub at Stoke Prior, saw a salt loader come in with two rose-decorated water cans. 'Plase be s'good as t'put two gallons in each and gie ma' a quart t'drink now.'

After a busy week of loading the 'lowance money' would mount up and then 'neither the foreman's cajolery or the manager's threats would induce them to do another stroke until every penny's worth had been drunk'.

Beer made great fighters of the boat people. At Stoke Prior, to the delight of many villagers, the boatmen at turning out time would proceed to 'fight each other fiercely to a standstill'.[13]

They were said to prefer 'beer to bibles and pugilism to parsons', but one man of the cloth at least had their measure. The Reverend Elijah Clarke came across two burly boatmen at the Worcester Wharf, Birmingham, 'with their coats off, their shirt sleeves rolled up . . . preparing for a fight'. Clarke rushed to put himself between them and ordered, 'You must not fight; you will hurt each other.'

'Get out of the way mister,' they growled.

'No! You will not fight while I am here.'

There they were trying to dodge round the intrepid parson, whirling their fists ineffectually at each other. The ludicrousness of the situation was soon apparent. Onlookers and fighters alike burst out laughing. The men put down their fists, put on their coats and went off with their boats in a friendly way.[14]

Even braver was the American missionary who came, by chance, upon a much more serious scenario. Two boats had collided and the crews of two more boats had been drawn into the battle which immediately flared up. Stones had already been thrown, a towrope cut and the crews were advancing upon each other armed with clubs, boat hooks and knives. 'At the risk of his life the missionary rushed between them, and by an eloquent appeal calmed the fury of the warriors and averted bloodshed.'

It is interesting to compare the boatmen of these two countries since they seemed to have much in common. The Americans too were said to be a 'hard-swearing, hard-drinking, hard-fighting lot'. Deacon Mason who began work on the Erie Canal in the early 1840s 'did not suppose there was another place in the world where there was as much iniquity'. The 'evils of rum' were, according to one report, at the bottom of much of it.[15]

Alcohol was not necessarily the cause of violence. Mr Hughes, representing the boatmen in a court case stemming from the long strike of Fellows, Morton & Clayton's workers in 1923, was not afraid to admit, 'These are somewhat of a tough class of men, and I do not think you can manage to eject them so very easily [from their boats]'.[16] And down through the years there is evidence enough to show that they were not men to be treated lightly. A word out of place to some boatmen could have unpleasant results, as when John Cherry, a canal clerk at Braunston, remonstrated one summer's evening in 1813 with Thomas Harris for 'beating and abusing his horse in a Cruel Manner'. Harris 'immediately collared him threatened to put him into the canal and then kicked him several times and tore his Cloathes very much'.[17] George Tavernor was another who spoke out of turn. He was the subject of 'a most violent and outrageous assault' from Thomas Dawson.[18] In one incident 'of the utmost brutality' witnesses confessed themselves afraid to stop it, 'the desperate temper of the boatmen being too well known'.

It could be a rough tough world on the canals in their heyday. The boatmen were paid piece rates. Those who made the most rapid passage made the most money. On the other hand the canal system was subject to delays; at locks, where great 'blocks' of boats built up; at loading and unloading points; at stoppages, for repairs, through drought or frost. This led to fretful scenes at some of these pressure points, and canal boating often involved a measure of 'physical negotiation'. William Bentley and James Watkin, two of Robert Williamson's boatmen, for example, battled it out over who should load first at Tunstall Bridge in 1840.

Sometimes they 'negotiated' not with fists but with their 70ft boats. John Carden was peacefully steering a limestone boat along the Trent & Mersey Canal towards Etruria Lock in 1839. He passed the distance post 10 yards from the lock which then gave him priority. Bryan Bennett, close behind, would have none of it and in his determination to get his boat into the lock first 'drove it with such force against . . . Carden's boat as caused it to sink'.[19]

The fly-boats in arrogantly taking precedence over other vessels —'stealing the road'—made many enemies. They did not always get their way. Two horses strained the sloop *Freedom*, heavily laden with corn, towards the Thwaite Lock on the Aire & Calder Navigation in 1831. A peremptory horn blast from behind signalled a hurrying fly-boat's intention to pass. The sloop should have moved away from the towpath and allowed the towrope to slacken so that the fly-boat could pass over it, but William Robinson, the master, had got out of bed on the wrong side. He visualized the fly-boat passing through and setting the lock against him.

'You shan't go past if I can help you!' he shouted back as the *Dispatch* approached, turning the sloop towards the towpath to block the fly-boat's passage.

Moore, the captain of the *Dispatch*, lightly loaded with 7 tons of wool from Goole, swung his rudder over to pass on the outside, aiming to lift his towrope over the sloop.

'If that rope comes over me, I'll cut it,' Robinson cried out, and sure enough he caught the rope, held it down until he laid his hand on a knife and sawed through it, leaving the fly-boat to drift helplessly in mid channel.[20]

What often happened was that as two competing 7ft 'narrow' boats, say, converged rapidly into a lock entrance about 7ft across, neither captain prepared to give way, there was a limit to how far they could penetrate before scraping to a halt, stuck fast like a cork in a bottle—'jammed'. Hence Mr Whitehouse was informed, 'That on 14 April 1813 John Heritage your Servant in endeavouring to take the turn of Smiths Robert Boat at the Locks . . . prevented the Boats passing One Hour' and 'That on the 18 Inst. He the S^d John Heritage by similar endeavour to take the turn of Isaac Parkes stop'd the passage of the Canal two hours'.[21]

It was always happening. Altercation and obstinacy could lengthen the time of stoppage. At Stoke Bruerne top lock, for instance, early one Monday morning in the 1870s, two steam

DON'T.

A Word to Our Canal-Boatmen.

DON'T waste the company's water by drawing the paddles before the gate is well shut.

· · · ·

DON'T "jam" a lock to spite your neighbour. It is like the dog in the manger, who would not eat the hay himself, nor would he let the horse eat it. Better give way and be happy.

· · · ·

DON'T urge your horse unduly, in order to be first at the lock. Such a race does the animal more harm in ten minutes than will a whole, but steady, day's work.

· · · ·

DON'T swear at your horse, your donkey, your wife or child—when you are vexed. At such a time it would be a good thing to pause, and count fifty; a better thing to laugh and be merry; best of all to pray.

· - · ·

DON'T be unkind to the animals when they seem to be a bit stupid. Ill-treatment kills the spirit of a horse, and renders him unfit for work. A good pat on the neck, and a kind word will do more to make the noble brute go than either a kick or a blow.

· · · ·

DON'T work hard day and night, and then take your earnings to the sign of the "Pig and Whistle." If you do, I fear the publican will get the pig, and you and your family will get the whistle. And a very sorry tune it will play.

· · · ·

DON'T say you will never sign the pledge again because you have broken it once. Sign it again if you have broken it a score times. Like a drowning man clutch at anything you think will save you. Seek the help of God, and you will overcome the power of strong drink.

· · · ·

DON'T stay away from church or chapel because your "best things" happen to be lying in the drawer at home. Come as you are. God looks at the heart and not at the garment. A poor coat or a shabby bonnet will never keep man or woman out of heaven, but a bad heart and a guilty conscience will.

E. Clarke.

Fig 1 'A Word to Our Canal Boatmen' from *The Waterman* implies that boatmen were still far from perfect in the twentieth century

tugs and their loaded barges disputed the right of way. According to the Grand Junction Company's by-laws the Fellows Morton pair had precedence, but the London & Birmingham Steam Company's man was in the lock first with his tug and refused to give way. The dispute dragged on. A 'block' of sixty boats soon built up, but it made no difference. The situation became quite humorous when the stubborn captain did finally give permission for his tug to be pulled out. For he and his men were playful people.

> A rope was fastened to the boat and the men began to pull, but the engine driver of the London and Birmingham Company's steamer jumped into the hold and put on full steam. Of course the efforts of those who attempted to pull the boat from the lock were unavailing and they were compelled to relinquish their task.

Word of the goings on had got about and a large crowd gathered in the hope of seeing 'a disturbance', but they were disappointed. Beyond exchanging 'frequent remarks of a bantering and sarcastic description' the sixteen boatmen saw the business through peacefully enough. Eventually, just before six on the Tuesday morning, after twenty-four hours of delay, Fellows Morton's boats were allowed to proceed.[22]

One can understand that such disputes were not always settled amicably and that subsequent meetings of the parties were not always peaceful. Mr Clarke, the fight stopper, had seen in his time 'a good deal of quarrelling and not a little fighting, on the canal side'.

'Fighting was one of the besetting sins of the canallers' in the USA too, according to Alvin Harlow and for much the same reasons—'The boat first through the lock was the boat whose crew could lick the other crew'. Captains often chose their men according to their fighting ability. It was not only an occupational hazard, but something of a pastime—there was not a great deal else to do. Warring crews would tie up their barges and continue a fight first started as a lock dispute weeks, even years, before. 'When one side cried "enough" they separated and went on their way as if nothing had happened.'

Some boatmen achieved considerable fame as fighters. There

was the 'Tipton Slasher' in England and Ben Streeter the 'Rochester Bully' in the USA who made history when he licked the 'Buffalo Bully' after an hour's pugilism in Rochester Arcade.[23]

Even in recent times some boat people enjoyed a good fight. In the 1950s one mischievous boatman, bored with the common round, or paying off some old score, left a loaf of bread on the beam of a lock gate as he passed through.

'What's that for?' enquired a curious passing boater.

'It's for ——,' he replied naming another boatman. 'He's so lazy he can't even make enough to feed his wife and kids.'

Later in the same day the 'sneer word' reached its intended victim who immediately gunned his boat and 'butty' down the canal in hot pursuit of the sower of discord. On the way he came across the boats of several relatives, who also worked for the same firm, and they joined in the chase to avenge family honour. A posse of boats arrived at their employer's Midland depot and the furious families gathered on the wharf out for blood. A heated discussion took place in the course of which the original cause of the business seems somehow to have got lost to be replaced by a general concensus as to how underpaid they all were.

A short time afterwards a visitor opened the door of the manager's office to find him pinned to the floor, surrounded by angry boat people, one of whom was threatening him with a rusty bayonet. Quickly sizing up the situation the visitor murmured, 'I'll come back when you are not so busy,' and left, closing the door discreetly behind him. The manager did survive unscathed to enjoy telling the tale.

Not only were they drunken, quarrelsome and violent, they were, by all accounts, dishonest as well. It seems they were especially careless in their use of canal-side property. Canals, argued the *Chester Courant* were,

. . . subject to an incessant nuisance, arising from the characters of their navigators; their banks are the scene of plunder—their boats are slow but sure movers—pilferage is committed, and the thief is gone off noiselessly and unperceived and untraced.[24]

Some of the boatmen were said to be noted poachers. As a boat glided quietly along, it would slacken speed, and one of the men would jump off and run into the woods, gun in hand.' "Crack! Crack!" would be heard and down would come a fine pheasant or brace of partridge and before the gamekeeper would come up, the boatman would be on board, smoking his pipe, or whistling "Jim Crow", gun and game being carefully buried in the bowels of the boat.'

Myles Pennington, as a small boy in the 1820s, was once on the Lancaster Canal wharf when the fly-boat arrived. A man from the town sidled up to the captain. 'En yo got out?'

'I hi,' says the captain—'Ten pheasants.'

Every boat had a dog aboard who knew his job. On the *Mary Jane* it was Jack 'a brindled and most forbidding looking lurcher'. 'If I sees un after un 'are I ain't the man as'll stop un,' said Captain Jonah to his passenger in 'a friendly communicative spirit'.[25]

Nothing was safe from these depredators—game, fowl, eggs, fish and even sheep, not to mention clothes hung out to dry and the milk of cows grazing in the field. One boat hand told George Smith:

> . . . of a most shocking and cruel affair in connection with boating-life, and by no means an isolated one . . . times had been rather hard with them, and in order to have a feast and a change from herrings and turnips, it was agreed that one of their number should fetch a sheep—for which boatmen have a special liking—out of the fields they passed on their voyage. The sheep was fetched by the boatman, and to kill the poor thing they began to beat out its brains with a stone. After bursting and knocking one of the harmless and innocent creature's eyes out, some of the party began to relent and to say they would have nothing further to do with the matter; the poor animal was turned into the field in this battered and heart-rending condition, to either live or die . . . tumbling about . . . with one eye burst and the other protruding.[26]

If the horse lacked fodder, there was food all around for the taking—if you could get away with it. Mary Philips would have told you a thing or two about boatmen. Henry Taylor had taken the liberty of turning his boat horse into a field that she rented near the canal at Stoke. She was leading it off to the pound when Taylor met her and objected. He 'struck and kicked her' in the process. The Philips were not a lucky family. Three days later, son

James came across boatman Thomas Starkey's horse eating happily in their field. No sooner was the animal taken off to the pound when up came Starkey, who brought it out again and began to make off without so much as 'by your leave'. An 'altercation' ensued. Young James was treated to a specimen of 'physical force' and pitched over the high fence into the pound.[27]

Boatmen were still 'borrowing' eggs and other items in the twentieth century. One Stoke Prior boatman was heard boasting of the fine range of vegetables in his garden.

'Well thee should'st have,' retorted another. 'Thy garden stretches from Gloucester to Brummagem.'[28]

3
Plundering Propensities and Horrid Depravities

'It is not *externally* only that . . . [the boatman] is busy,' the *Chester Courant* went on, 'he lies by for the night . . . whilst his boat is loaded with useful commodities of all sorts—wine, spirits, tea, sugar, tobacco and other delectabilia which cheer and invigorate the homeless, nameless navigator and which if he do not himself consume, he has a customer for in every hamlet . . .'.

Respected Cheshire justices like the Reverend Henry Broughton, Trafford Traffords, and Francis Burton, would have agreed. They confirmed that the most common offences they had to deal with were perpetrated on the canals. There was a good deal of wool stealing according to Broughton. Traffords spoke of the numerous cases from petty theft up to the crime of murder that it had been his duty to investigate. Salt, which, with the excise duty on it, was a very valuable commodity, disappeared from flats between the Cheshire salt fields and Liverpool.[1] Earlier the Old Quay Company had complained of thefts from its Liverpool–Manchester merchandise flats.[2] Myles Pennington reckoned that at one time the pilferage of goods in transit on Lancashire canals became so organised that a shop was opened for their sale at Wigan.

It was not only in the north west that there was a problem. 'It appears, in fact,' wrote Patrick Colquhoun in 1800, 'that the immense Property which floats upon navigable Rivers and Canals in all quarters is become subject to waste and Depredation in a very great degree.'[3] It was 'a subject of complaint throughout the kingdom', and it still was in 1839 when goods were equally at risk from the 'plundering propensities of these free-booters'.

Traffords was good enough to suggest reasons for canals being 'one of the greatest causes of crime in the county'. He attributed it 'most particularly to the want of due observance of the Sunday; for as they work upon that day, they seem to have no rudder, moral or religious, for their guidance'. The boatmen were also, he added, 'induced to it by a number of very powerful receivers'— 'outside harpies' Pennington called them.

Boatmen used small collapsible copper pumps to draw out a large quantity of spirits in a very short time from the casks aboard in which a hole had been drilled under the hoop. Water was quickly pumped back in to make up the loss, the hole sealed and the hoop knocked back into place. When the loss was discovered, perhaps many weeks later, it was difficult to trace the culprits, the cask having passed through so many hands. It was almost impossible to catch the boatmen in the act, which might have taken place on a moving boat under a tarpaulin in the middle of a dark night. There might be suspicions held against a boatman; it was another matter to secure a conviction.

Sometimes, however, the robbers were 'blown' by one of their own number. The inspection of a puncheon of rum and a hogshead of brandy just unloaded at a wharf on the Chesterfield Canal in 1841 revealed that the spirits were not 'in accordance with the standard sample taken in Stockwith'. The crew of the boat were questioned and William Bell, one of the hands, spilled the beans. At Misterton Bottom Lock, George Ellis, the captain, had left his brother, Thomas, and Bell to work the boat up through the locks. By the time they reached the top lock Ellis was back with Richard Fox, a 'fence' who lived in Misterton. They disappeared into the hold with two bottles. For nearly an hour they trafficked among the groceries, 'smuggling' out two gallons of rum and a gallon of brandy altogether. Then £1 changed hands. Bell, who was probably not a regular member of the crew, was bought off with 10s and further implicated by being asked to take the incriminating tools—a gimlet, a syphon and a funnel— to Ann Smith's. Bell's evidence got Ellis and Fox sent down for twelve months' hard labour.[4]

Others were caught and sentenced. William Riley and John Jones served two months for stealing earthenware from the crates in one of the Anderton Carrying Company's boats which they worked. William Furnival admitted to delivering only part of a boatload of building materials in Wolverhampton. The rest, valued at almost £5, he had sold elsewhere. John Lakey hired a boat and then tried to sell it many miles away. John Broadfield went to great lengths to cover up his theft of the 'tonnage money' —17s 0½d—given to him by his Wolverhampton employers to pay for tolls and other expenses. At Nantwich he sank the boat![5] Thomas Cordwell, while ostensibly loading his boat with coal on the Chesterfield Canal, was surreptitiously slipping in over a ton of valuable pig iron. Suspicions were aroused when he tried to sell it in Boston. He hid the boat and its 'hot' cargo in a quiet drain of the fens, but the police sniffed it out.[6]

Complaints and culprits seemed to lessen from the 1840s, although one agent did mention in 1875 that there was 'an element of pilferage in the canal traffic'. And Sam Lomas, Autherley lock-keeper, used to relate the story of Billy Biggerton, who, during World War I, made a delivery of rationed sugar. 'All the sugar dry, Billy?' asked the agent.

'Every bit of it. It's as sweet as honey.'

'How do you know it's as sweet as honey?' the agent demanded. 'Have you been pilfering?'

'You've nothin' to worry at gaffer,' replied Billy with a sly grin. 'If you worked in a snuff factory would you buy your own snuff.?'[7]

There were some rare characters among the canal staff too and some dishonest ones. Toll-collectors embezzled tolls; lock-keepers indulged in shady transactions with boatmen; porters pilfered. There was a certain rough justice about the activities of some porters on the Lancaster Canal. A number of wool bags down from Scotland had lost their marks and remained unclaimed in the Preston warehouse. These were being moved into a store-room when one of the porters laid himself down on the bags and felt something hard. 'There's a dead man in that bag!' he cried, jumping up.

They opened it. Not a body but a 10 gallon keg of Scotch whisky was hauled out. It was being smuggled into England without paying revenue. The porters 'confiscated' the whisky and 'were not fairly sober for a month afterwards'.[8]

Labourers and lengthsmen had less opportunity to be dishonest, but things did 'fall off a boat and valuable items were sometimes found about the canal. In July 1806 the Worcester & Birmingham Company had to 'severly reprimand the workmen who sold the pig iron they found in the locks some time ago at Camp Hill'.

One of the rarest characters described by Pennington was Johnny Morrison, John Hargreaves' wharfinger at Tewitfield on the Lancaster Canal. He went with his father to examine the Scotsman's books.

Johnny was a bachelor and lived in a little den above his office. Boy-like I peeped into the domicile. There was a small fire grate which from appearances had not been cleaned out for many days; the ashes and cinders were about to enter the bed which stood close by. Johnny did his own cooking, but he did not do anything else towards house-keeping and the place looked as if it would have been all the better if feminine hands had had a little to do with it. The office desk below had a layer of dust upon it, carefully preserved, the disturbance of which by a broom would have driven the auditor out of the office, but Johnny took a rag and shoved the dust on one side forming a sort of square of earth works for the cash book.

Johnny had an original method of balancing his cash book. He only added up the credit side, and made the debit side agree with it, regardless of all rules of arithmetic . . .

'Why how's this?' said father, 'the addition is incorrect.'

Johnny: 'It's a'reet, mon, dinna ye ken th'coont balances on baith sides.'

There was a considerable shortage of cash and Johnny's wharfage business 'came to a sudden close'.

'Bominableness did not encompass drunkenness, violence and dishonesty alone. Other, and worse affairs were afoot upon the waterways.

'Murder! Murder!' screamed Elizabeth Clayton as she struggled to escape from the narrow cabin bed of a London-bound fly-boat in 1823. In a fit of lust Samuel Hodgkinson, the burly twenty-three year old captain, had swept the buxom young Irish woman onto the bed and had begun to take 'indecent liberties' with her. 'Is there no one to save me?' she cried out in despair.

'Nobody can save you,' grunted William Rawlinson who, along with Joseph Maxfield, another young member of the crew, was cynically watching.

'Father, what did you rear me for to be used so by these men?' the unfortunate woman gasped out. 'Good God Almighty deliver me from these men.'

'Your father nor God can't save you this time until I have done with you,' said Hodgkinson.

For a quarter of an hour Mrs Clayton fought to ward off the captain's evil intentions until, weak and hoarse from shouting, she was forced to submit when the two stout crewmen took hold of her to 'assist the monster in the commission of his vile purpose'.

Rawlinson then seized her with the intention of following his captain's example. She screamed, resisted anew and appealed to Hodgkinson to help her. At a word from the captain the hand did let her go. She escaped into the hold, but there was to be no shelter there. Driven out she climbed up on to the narrow top plank.

'God pity the stranger,' whimpered the unhappy Mrs Clayton as she sat in the cold night rain.

After a time Hodgkinson, who was steering, seemed to take pity on her and told her to go down into the cabin again and warm herself by the fire. She refused.

Hodgkinson then asked her to go with him to a stable and pass for his wife when they got to the Islington tunnel.

'I'd rather throw myself in the canal,' she told him.

'I'll be damned if I will,' retorted the captain catching hold of her, 'but you may if you like, after I have done with you.'

'Oh my God,' she cried out, 'you are not going to kill me again.'

He pushed her down until her head was almost in the water and 'repeated his former crime'.[9]

That was how it all happened according to Mrs Clayton when she later charged the three men with rape and it is no more than one might have expected from a class of men who were said to be 'entirely depraved'. For the sexual appetites of the boatmen were rumoured to be as unbridled as their other indulgences. When in London they were generally 'drawn into brothels' to 'associate with females of the worst description'. Or it was common for them to hire 'Females to accompany them say from London to Manchester and back again'.

Elizabeth Clayton was almost certainly not one these 'Females'. On the contrary she carried with her 'a certificate of character for quietness, sobriety, honesty and strict attention' given to her by Mrs Gelston of Cuffe Street, Dublin. She had been with Mrs Gelston as a domestic servant for nearly four years. But what was she doing aboard a moving canal boat on the outskirts of London?

She was looking for her husband, Mortimer, a carpenter, who, from necessity, had left her and was somewhere in London. Anxious to see him she got leave of Mrs Gelston and set out for Liverpool. From the port she walked south for three days to Stone in Staffordshire and there she paid 4s for her conveyance to London in a canal boat. After two days and nights aboard this boat she was transferred at Cowley Lock to Hodgkinson's vessel to take her the remaining 18 miles into London.

Though the comment of a Dorset man in 1847 that 'we very much vegetate where we are born, and live very close indeed', was probably a fair appraisal of English rural communities up to that time, there were many people like Elizabeth Clayton on the move to distant places long before the railways came.

It is true that the proportions of people who were attracted from afar to the new industrial areas were, logically enough, much less than those who came from nearby. But they did come none the less; a few from this distant county and some from that— to Lancashire, Yorkshire, Staffordshire and other growth areas. The call of London was heard and answered throughout the British Isles. *Proportionally* small, taken together, the *number* of workers who travelled over long distances in search of greener pastures was perhaps not insignificant. The restless Irish and Scots swelled their ranks. Hopeful emigrants made for the ports.

Given the will or the need to move, it was not really true to say, as Adam Smith did, that 'a man is of all sorts of luggage the most difficult to be transported'. He could move himself well enough as Charles Mott explained in 1844.

The Irish and other labourers, in seeking work, invariably walk their journeys, if ever so long; in this practice there is no altera-tion; it was the custom before the railways ... and it is still followed: in the season you may see hundreds of these industrious men on their journeys, walking barefooted, with their shoes under their arms, to lessen as much as possible the cost of their journey.

It was the appendages with which a man surrounded himself that restricted his mobility as much as anything. A wife and children and the effects that went with them could not tramp from one end of the kingdom to the other. Nor could they go by stage coach. It cost £6 2s for two adults and three children to travel between London and Manchester—an impossible price for a labouring man.

It is a little realised fact that many working people moved themselves and their chattels in canal boats. Not in the 'passage' boats specially built for passengers, which rapidly carried the relatively well-to-do over short distances, as on the Bridgewater Canal between Runcorn and Manchester, but in the everyday goods–carrying vessels.

'The poor who had to travel . . .', explained Rowland Price, a Staffordshire Poor Law official, 'frequently went by canal boat. The boat had no regular charge, and passengers were usually taken without the consent of the proprietors. The payment frequently consisted of what they called treating, giving beer and spirits at the various stations.'[10]

This is what Hodgkinson was about with Elizabeth Clayton. They were liable to a fine of one guinea but they still risked it. On the Lancaster Canal Hargreaves' fly-boats were under a penalty of £10 per man if they carried passengers, but, according to Pennington, 'the boatmen generally managed to stow two or three on board'. Accidents to Yorkshire keels often reveal that they were carrying passengers. Thomas Masterman, a Knottingley potter, was coming up from Goole aboard the fly-boat *Dispatch* when it tangled with William Robinson's sloop in 1831.

It was akin to the 'shouldering' of the coachmen and the 'cabbaging' of the waggoners—taking passengers without declaring them and pocketing a much reduced fare. It was even easier and cheaper on a canal boat.

Carrying passengers was not always an illicit trade. Many fly-boat companies carried them in the hold among the cargo on a regular and open basis. They were entered on the passage bill and paid a fixed charge. For much of the Canal Age it was 14s from Manchester to London, 16s from Liverpool, 7s or 8s from Lichfield—children half price. Slow though it was (five days from Manchester to London) it was smoother than a jostling waggon.

Catherine Lindon brought herself and five children to London this way in 1823, accompanied by her brother, Thomas Shaw, a labourer. They were natives of Killashee in Longford, Ireland. Boarding Hodgkinson's boat at Preston Brook, 20 miles to the south of Liverpool on Wednesday 30 July as regular passengers, they arrived in London early in the Monday morning, their journey not being without incident.

Rowland Price did add, 'decent females were wholly precluded from that mode of conveyance exposed as they would be, in the same cabin and without protection, to the society of men not proverbial for the respect with which under such circumstances they conduct themselves'.

One respectable voyager, a Kettering shoemaker, compelled to emigrate with his family through bankruptcy in 1823, would have agreed wholeheartedly. He travelled by canal boat from Leicester to Liverpool and in a letter from New York recalled how,

> . . . we were taken up the canel by a drunken set of Men for I think I never hard worse men to Sware and Curse then some of them it seemeth that the Lords day is the Day that they get Drunk and are not fitt for the duty they have to do so that we were near being upset at one of the locks.[11]

Christina Collins too would have endorsed such complaints—had she lived.

In May 1839 Robert Collins had gone to London in search of work. Obtaining a job as an ostler he was soon able to send a sovereign to his wife in Liverpool, so that she could join him.

One pound would not buy a rail ticket. Accordingly Mrs Collins paid the 16s to travel by Pickfords. At 7 o'clock on Saturday night, 15 June, having crossed the Mersey, she stood on the wharf at Preston Brook, with two boxes and a bundle, waiting for the London fly-boat—a small active-looking woman of thirty-six, obviously poor, but wearing clothes that were clean and in good repair.

The boat pulled in. Mrs Collins may have had a foreboding of disaster when she realised that she was to be the only passenger, for on boarding the boat she told the three burly boatmen that if any one 'mislested' her she would 'make herself away'.

Off they went down the Trent & Mersey Canal. Soon she found that the travelling conditions in the hold of the fly-boat were to be more uncomfortable than she had anticipated. She complained to the captain that it was 'very hard for her to have paid sixteen shillings and to have no straw'.

Food was another problem. Again she had to approach the captain—James Owen, a hearty middle-aged man. If he would but find her 'victuals' she promised that he would be 'satisfied' when they got to London.

Owen clearly thought that she would be able to satisfy him long before then. Giving his first hand—twenty-seven year old George Thomas—6d to *leg* the boat through Barnton tunnel (near Northwich) in his place, he invited her, against company regulations, into the warm cabin. Given the alternative in the hard, cold hold she was not loathe to accept. In conversation he learned and clearly misconstrued the information that she had theatrical connections—she was actually a dressmaker. Sufficiently encouraged, his misconceived hopes again led him to get someone else—'a man who was about'—to leg through the Harecastle tunnel for 1s.

Whatever happened in the cabin during the passage through the tunnels Mrs Collins was sufficiently anxious to express some concern to William Brookes, one of Pickfords' porters, when the fly-boat arrived at Stoke around Sunday noon. Thomas and the other hand, twenty-eight year old William Ellis, who were both said later to be of the most 'depraved and profligate character', apparently *thought* that Owen had been successful in his amorous intentions. Ellis reckoned that they were 'uncommonly friendly', and Thomas remarked to a passing boatman 'Jemmy had concerns with her last night'. He intended to follow suit. At Stoke he began to press his attentions upon the tremulous Mrs Collins.

'Leave me alone,' she cried. 'I'll have nothing to do with you.'

After unloading and loading the three men adjourned to John Mackey's beer shop leaving the sixteen year old boat boy William Musson in charge of the boat. Unaccountably the woman went with them, perhaps to eat. The men drank about seven pints of porter between them. She drank nothing.

They left Stoke at 4 o'clock. Mrs Collins looked tired, troubled and poorly. The men were not drunk, but their appetite for

48

alcohol had been sharpened sufficiently for them to *smuggle* whisky from the cask in the hold.

When the vessel pulled alongside the Stone Wharf at 8 o'clock that evening a concerned young woman could be seen anxiously tying up her bundle ready to jump out. The canal company's clerk, Hugh Cordwell, persuaded her to stay where she was until he had gauged the boat. Clambering out she explained to him that the crew were drunk and how afraid she was of what they might do to her. Cordwell had already observed the condition of the men for himself. The inebriate state of Owen was particularly evident.

Mrs Collins walked over to a nearby bridge to assess her position, but Owen lurched after her and suggested that she go with him through the town. In disgust she went quickly away from him under the bridge. None the less she was back on the boat when it left ten minutes later.

As dusk fell the crew of the fly-boat met up with Thomas Bloor and his men near Sandon Lock heading north with the *Emma* and the *Gleddy's*. Owen and Thomas joined Bloor in his cabin for a quick glass of ale. Something (probably illicit whisky) was passed from Owen to Bloor. 'Will you have anything of this?' Owen pointed to the woman.

'No, I have no inclination,' Bloor wisely replied and went on his way.

Shortly after leaving Sandon Lock, passion and alcohol finally tore away the men's restraint—'at the best but very feeble'—and they began to be rough with the woman. She managed to escape onto the towpath and soon ran out of sight.

They came up with her again at Shirleywich Lock, a mile or so down the canal, where she was in earnest conversation with the lock-keeper's wife. Fearing that the men would molest her, she was apprehensive about going further with them.

But she did go. No doubt the fact that she was hungry, cold, penniless, miles from anywhere and alone in a dark alien world just finely tipped the scales against abandoning the boat voyage.

She continued to walk along the towpath, but Ellis and Thomas got out of the boat and kept 'mauling her all the way'. Nearing midnight, just before Hoo Mill Lock, Mrs Collins was finally overpowered. . . .

The violated woman was dragged back to the boat, but her

terrified screams awoke the lock-keeper, James Mills, and his wife Ann. She described what happened.

'I heard a noise at the lock—a cry, I thought as if somebody was abusing a child—a cry of distress. I got up and opened the window. A boat of Pickfords was in the lock. [I knew it was Pickford's boat by the letter board. They are large white letters different to any of the other boats.] . . . I saw [a woman] at the top of the cabin . . . with her legs hanging on the outside. There were three men with the boat.

"Don't attempt me. I'll not go down," she cried, "I'll not go in there."

"What woman is that with you?" I called to the man under the window.

"A passenger."

"Is there anybody with her?"

"Her husband."'

With this reply Mrs Mills seems to have been satisfied.

Ellis and Thomas now began to work the boat. The boy was asleep. Mrs Collins lay on the cross bed when Owen entered the cabin.

'Oh Captain! Captain!' she vainly implored him. 'What shall I do? Oh my Collins! my Collins! I wish you were here!'

Owen admitted later that he then 'tried to have to do with her but could not'.

At Colwich Lock it was the turn of Owen and the boy to go to work and the others to go to bed. Owen recalled,

Being drunk with the whiskey or one thing and another I was very loathe to get up, but I did get up. The boy went to drive the horse; I steered the boat. The other two were in the cabin [with] the woman. They got the bottle to have some more whiskey and while they were having it the woman slipped out of the cabin into the hatches where I was. She made an attempt to get out of the boat and got her legs halfway into the water. I leaned over and pulled her out. They pulled her into the cabin again where they committed rapes upon her and completely mauled her to death. . . . What made them do it was they knew what they had been doing with her, and she would tell.

When the act was done the men began to quarrel. Eventually

the captain took the dead woman out and laid her on the top of the cabin.

At around one-thirty in the morning the problem of what to do with the body was solved, when on taking the sharp turn at Brindley's Bank near Rugeley, the lurch of the boat tumbled Christina Collins into the water.

The four boatmen were subsequently arrested at Fazeley and sent for trial, although the charges against the boy were later dropped. Owen, Thomas and Ellis were first tried for rape, but acquitted through insufficient evidence. This trial, held at Stafford, witnessed a particularly poignant moment when,

Robert Collins . . . entered the witness box in a great state of excitement and distress. He wept aloud, and seemed as if he could hardly bear the sight of the prisoners at the bar. [He was able to identify his wife's body] for although it was dreadfully disfigured— (here the poor fellow could not all restrain his feelings) yet he knew it by a mark on the ear.

The trial for murder was postponed until the following March when, with the evidence of the prosecution strengthened by the testimony of Joseph Orgill, the three boatmen were found guilty.

The processes of law were duly enacted, though not quite so fully as had been intended, for one of the prisoners was missing from the scaffold. Part of this reconstruction is based upon Orgill's summary of Owen's conversation with him in prison. It will be seen that the master comes out of the affair rather well, having taken part in neither the murder nor the rape. From later events it seems clear that Owen played a more sinister role. Much of the part supposedly played by Ellis was in fact probably perpetrated by Owen, although Ellis did later acknowledge having attempted to violate Mrs Collins, but he had failed in his object. In any event the sentence on Ellis was commuted to transportation for life.

The incident did nothing to improve the already tarnished image of the canal world. Enemies of the boat people, of which there were many, revelled in accounts of 'scenes which are of daily occurrence among boatmen'. The 'depraved and profligate' habits of Owen, Thomas and Ellis did not differ 'much from those of the class of men to which they belonged', it was said.[12]

4

I Will Go and Be a Boatman

They were a rum lot it seems. Where did they come from this peculiar race of people? In 1920 Owen Llewellyn, the canal boat inspector, reckoned 'Boat people are born not made. I have yet to come across any of them who have come on water from any other occupation', and it is true that by the later nineteenth century boating was very much a self-perpetuating occupation.[1] But where did the very first watermen come from?

There was in fact a great deal of continuity in the peopling of even the earliest waterways. As 'navigations' and broad canals were built in the eighteenth century to allow the penetration of craft further inland from such estuaries and rivers as the Mersey, Severn, Humber, Trent and Thames, it was the existing flats, trows, keels, billy boys, sloops, barges and wherries which came to use them. Such waterways as the Mersey & Irwell and Weaver Navigations and the Sankey Canal, for instance, brought the commerce of Manchester, the salt of Northwich and the coal of St Helens within navigable reach of the long-navigable Mersey estuary, Liverpool and the sea. Humber vessels could get up into West Yorkshire by the Aire & Calder and then other navigations.

More flatmen and keelmen were needed, of course, but much of this increased demand was met on the principle of heredity. Sons followed fathers onto such craft, and there were more sons either because more were born or less died or both; no one is really certain.

These were the descendants of those brave mariners who had first ventured upon the rivers centuries before and the exact origins of the earliest watermen will no doubt remain one of the secrets of history, although the similarity of many of the river and coastal craft to the Viking long boat raises the possibility that flatmen and keelmen were directly descended from the Norsemen. Connections with the open sea continued. Whether it was generally the practice for mariners to renounce the sea for work on calmer inland waters, or whether work on the flats and keels tempted some to venture abroad in ocean-going ships is not clear. Some alternated from one to the other.

John Maddock of Hale was both sailor and flatman in the eighteenth century, although his son was described as a flatman only.[2] Thomas Catterall had been little more than a child in 1775 when he first left his land home. By 1795 he was master of the *Peter and Sarah* working the coal-salt triangle. He also had experience on the Old Quay and the Duke's flats as well as in the coasting trade until, in 1805, he became master of a 'black flat', working between Liverpool and Runcorn for the next twenty years. But he 'once went to China and back'.[3] Many had an unexpected taste of sea air, seasoned perhaps with the smell of burning powder, between 1793 and 1815 when they rallied or were pressed to the service of the colours. John Askew proudly recounted his years spent on a twenty gunner.[4]

There was another connection with the sea in that many billy boys, sloops, and 'outside' flats (ie those going outside the Mersey Bar) and even some keels worked not only over inland waterways, but were also coastal craft navigating the North and Irish Seas.

Many an old salt was to be found on river craft. One master of a Medway barge which regularly passed up the Regent's Canal had spent forty years in such vessels. Before that he had been in the navy, although he had perhaps not been a great success as a sailor. He was a cantankerous old ex-tar, but his daughter made allowances for him.

Father do grumble a good bit; but you see he is very old, and he don't mean no harm, and we don't take no notice. Why he left the navy 'cos he was so tender-'arted; he couldn't a-bear to do no'arm to no one and so when they put him as a guard over four or five prisoners as 'ad deserted and been caught, he lets 'em all go, one at a time, while he pretended not to be lookin'; they was all caught agin; yet he was allers in dread after that, and so he left. And he was admiral's fisherman, too, he was.[5]

On the canals proper there would seem to have been a complete

break with the past. Men were needed to take up an occupation completely new to these inland areas. Yet even here there was continuity, though of a different sort.

In Cheshire, before the canals, the transportation of goods was in the hands of 'many farmers and poor people who now chiefly subsist by Land Carriage . . .'.[6] It was not only in Cheshire, but all over the country that small tenant farmers were involved in land carriage on a part-time basis. When canal promotion was afoot, advice was offered to these carriers that they would do better, 'instead of driving waggons learn to steer and navigate a boat'.[7] That is exactly what many of them seem to have done.

They did not really need the advice. The building of a canal required vast quantities of materials: bricks, stones, timber and clay. Spoil was thrown up which had to be carried away. Who would carry these items but the men who always did the carrying in that locality? When the first section of the canal was finished and flooded, boats (provided by the company) instead of carts began to supply materials to the construction areas. Out of the cart shafts came the horse and off he went, perhaps unwillingly at first, pulling the boat at the end of a long line.

When the canal was fully opened these carriers and their horses stayed with the boats transporting the farm produce, coal, limestone, iron and other goods previously carried in their carts and waggons.

American farmers were in at the start of canal transport too according to Alvin Harlow. 'In the early days of the Erie and some of the other canals', he wrote, 'many farmers and other producers built each his own boat and carried his own produce to market with the assistance of one or two hands. Later the carrying business fell more into the hands of professional boatmen. . . .'

Plates 5 and 6 Flats and Keels: (above) Mersey sailing flats in Canning Dock, Liverpool c 1908. They were relatively few by then. Sailing vessels were more numerous on the Yorkshire waterways and were a common sight well into the inter-war years because conditions there were more suitable (the late Edward Jones); (below) sailing keels head up the Stainforth & Keadby Canal from Keadby lock on the Trent (Lincolnshire Library Service)

In England it may well have been that it was the part-time carrier-farmers who became the professional boatmen (usually in other people's boats) gradually giving up their farms as distances lengthened and trade quickened.

Why did the carrier move so easily into boating? On the one hand it seemed the natural thing to do, but, far more persuasively, he did it because the money was good. Before the canals farmer-carriers were said to get 'but mean and poor livelyhoods'. In contrast some of the men boating during the construction of the Birmingham Canal were making large sums of money; Job Lloyd averaged £2 1s 10d a week over sixteen weeks in 1771; James Jukes £3 13s 9d a week over seven weeks; others earned a steady £1 14s.[8]

Of course there were the capital and running costs of the horse to be met—about 10s a week. Unfortunately too, it was found that a 70ft—30 ton—boat would not follow the horse in the same obedient way that the traditional cart had done. There was much bumping and scraping in the early days. A helm had to be fixed and someone had to be paid to hold it while the carrier drove the horse. No matter, a lad could be had for 3s or 4s a week—seventy years later young Joseph Johnson could only get 2s 6d out of John Smith, although his mother insisted that the boatman had promised 3s 6d.[9] There were probably other minor expenses—ropes, etc—but many of these men were taking home close on £1 a week, and sometimes more, at a time when agricultural labourers could expect to get 7–9s.

Job Lloyd and others like him continued boating when the Birmingham Canal was fully opened to Autherley in 1772. In fact they made it a life's work. Their names crop up in canal company minute books and letters and many of them are listed in the register of boats and boatmen drawn up in 1795. Some names on the register also appear in the Land Tax Assessments as owners or tenants of land. The farming connection was a persistent one.

The first boatmen were not drawn exclusively from farmer-carriers. The job was open to anyone who could lay hands on a horse, though sometimes they must also 'produce Certificates of their Sobriety and Honesty'. Some navvies—local labourers who had earned enough to buy a horse; or ageing itinerant professionals, wearying of the wandering life—were almost certainly among those who took to the boats.

By the same token some of the canal-builders remained behind when the cut was complete to maintain their work and see to the smooth running of the waterway. The Birmingham & Liverpool Junction Canal Committee proposed, in July 1834, that the lock-keepers and bank tenders (lengthsmen) should be recruited almost exclusively from the workmen building the canal. Lock-keepers were to be drawn mainly from craftsmen and foremen. The bank tenders were to be 'selected from the most sober, steady and experienced persons . . . employed upon the works—Foremen or steady, sober labourers'. It was a sensible and long-established practice. As the second part of the Birmingham Canal was nearing completion in July 1772, it was decided that John Brown, a carpenter, would be the lock-keeper at Wolverhampton. An edge-tool maker, Isaac Parkes, was also recommended to be a lock-keeper. It was quite common in the Canal Age, especially on the smaller canals, for a man to carry out two (and even more) functions, like Thomas Bennet, appointed engine worker, blacksmith and lock-keeper on the Barnsley Canal at 'Bargh' in 1802.

Charles Bate came to canal work by chance. The regular blacksmith on the works of the Worcester & Birmingham Canal fell ill and the contractors turned to him at his smithy near Stoke Prior to sharpen and harden the masons' and bricklayers' tools and shoe the canal horses. The sick smith never returned to work; Charles Bate carried on and began a pattern of employment which saw the Bate family working on canal maintenance in one capacity or another for the next century and a half.[10]

Evidence of the origins of canal tradesmen like Charles Bate, and of those who came to fill more exalted positions, is sparse. Their names are preserved, but rarely their pedigree. It would be surprising if carpenters, toll-collectors, wharfingers and the like were not often chosen from men who had proved their worth during the building of the canal. Very often, however, the more responsible posts were filled by advertising. The Birmingham Committee ordered that 'a proper person be advertised for to superintend and conduct the Wharf at the termination of the Canal near Birmingham', and an advertisement did appear for 'a sober, diligent man'. Who was taken on is not clear, but the job of wharfinger soon devolved upon Richard Hipkiss, small farmer and failed waterway carrier, who seems to have been taken on mainly as a way of ensuring that money owed by him to the company was paid off. It was to be a disappointment if that was the aim since he died leaving his debts intact.[11] In any event it is unlikely that he was a typical recruit.

Companies continued to advertise and men were drawn from all walks of life. Richard Leaf, a railway clerk, was appointed lock-keeper on the Market Weighton Canal in 1862.[12] Joseph Nokes, appointed wharfinger at Leicester in 1861, had been an upholsterer by trade and he got the job in preference to a grocer, a clerk in a tax office and a book-keeper.[13]

Increasingly, however, the labour force became self-perpetuating. Sons followed fathers if not into the same position then into other canal jobs. Myles Pennington, the son of Hargreaves' agent on the Lancaster Canal, started his canal life in 1830 as a sixteen year old clerk apprenticed for five years in Hargreaves' Preston fly-boat office. Pennington went on to higher things and of course posts were often filled by promotion—a clerk became toll-collector or agent; an able porter might become warehouseman. In March 1776 Charles Sharratt, 'who was warehouseman to Henshall and Co', offered himself as wharfinger to the Birmingham Company.

Many men were content to stay with one company, even in the same job, for many years—all their life often—and a surprising number seemed to live a long life. In 1841 the gauging clerk at Hillmorton retired after nearly fifty years in the service of the Oxford Canal Company. Griffith Griffith, a labourer on the Neath Canal since 1791, was still at work in 1840. Men still toiling on in their seventies and even eighties are everywhere to be found, usually after a life-time of service with one company. 'One thing that struck us', wrote P. Bonthron after a cruise along the Kennet & Avon Canal in the years before World War I, 'was the fact of their long term of service, as we were told that nearly all the men had been on the same duty from twenty to forty years—truly a remarkable record.'

Another source of recruitment for land staff lay among the boaters. William Boaz, the thirteen year old son of a boatman, was a clerk in the Chester canal office in 1871.[14] There was 'J. Rogers, boatman, having proved himself suitable—to be put on the staff' of the Shropshire Union in 1885.[15] Ageing watermen, after years of steady service, were often given a shore job as the work aboard began to get too much for them. An old man in charge of a lock at Runcorn in 1910 told his life story in a few words.

> I wor born on the canal—on the canal boat in a Shropshire valley. I wor never eddicated, never went to school. I pulled at the rope on the tow-path when I were a baby a' most. The canal an' the boat an' the hawse ha' been my mates always—I married a boat girl—a real woman she was in her way, stronger ner a horse. I have three sons an' two daughters on the canals o' England somewhere—married, an' have children o' their own. The canal has been my world, my life. When I got too old to tug at the rope, they made me into a lock-keeper, an' here I am till God wants me![16]

Henry Brookes, a bad lock-keeper at Knostrop was superseded, 'for habitual inebriety and neglect of his duties', by Thomas Glover 'many years an active and steady Sloop Master' in the service of the Aire & Calder Navigation Company.[17]

Sons continued to follow fathers onto the vessels too as the waterways expanded, but there were not enough. The fact is that from the 1790s there was a tremendous expansion in waterway activity. The 2,223 miles of navigable river and canal of 1790 had grown to 3,456 by 1810. The number of vessels increased equally dramatically with the system and with quickening trade. The Mersey fleet of flats, for instance, which comprised about 180 craft in 1788 had risen to over 600 by 1826. There was an even greater expansion on the canals proper. Demands for labour could no longer be met by the traditional hereditary processes.

All sorts of people were drawn onto the vessels. Farm labourers, or more usually their sons, were the most common recruits especially in the early days. In particular, George Thomas began his passage to the gallows from a farm labourer's cottage in Wombourn when, at sixteen, he took to the boats. As industry developed, recruitment increasingly reflected the greater diversity of the economy. Not surprisingly men moved onto the waterways from industries which were closely involved with the vessels. A salt-boiler like John Musgrove (b 1805), a carpenter's son, was no doubt tempted down the Weaver by tales of adventure and romance and the money to be earned by the crews of the flats loading at the salt manufactory where he worked. Such industries had often grown dramatically in a short space of years, thus attracting many newcomers to work there. Once the roots of these people had been pulled up, their inhibitions to further change were weakened.

Recruits came from the most unlikely trades. John and James Plumb were the sons of a wealthy Northwich weaver turned salt trader. James Percival had been a shoemaker before turning flatman, a fatal decision since he was drowned in 1840. The sons of a shipwright, a boilermaker and a weaver; an apprentice framework knitter, an apprentice wheelwright and a whitewasher were among those who found their way on to the water in the early nineteenth century. As late as 1861 it is still possible to find the sons of farm labourers, carpenters, coalminers, brass-tap founders and bricklayers taking to the boats.[18]

There were two main reasons why such people took up this new life. The first was that the money or the opportunities were good, especially on the keels and flats; the second was that the men and boys were escaping, sometimes because of something bad they had done on land. In 1796 the basic wage of the first hand on board a Liverpool–Manchester merchandise flat was 13s plus various bonuses. In that same year a porter in Manchester was earning 11s and even a carpenter earned only 14s.[19] The Weaver hands would earn slightly less. Wages in Yorkshire would be comparable according to the goods carried. Earnings on these 'wide' vessels continued to compare very favourably with shore workers throughout the Canal Age.

Little is known of the wages paid to hands on the narrow canals in the eighteenth century. They were less than on the flats and keels, but the indications are that they compared reasonably well with labouring jobs on shore. In any event career prospects were good in a rapidly expanding trade. Many captains were young. In the 1820s and 1830s wages were around 8s with 'maintenance' which lifted earnings marginally above those of the agricultural labourers who toiled in the fields through which the canals passed.

Given such inducements it is surprising that the waterways became a settling ground for ''bominable bad uns', the more so since for most of the eighteenth century there were relatively few complaints made against the watermen, although examples can always be found of the independent spirit of captains and of the occasional drunken or dishonest indiscretion on the part of the hands. By all accounts they were generally respectable and respected people, forceful but not wicked.

Between about 1790 and 1815 the waterways got indigestion. The war caused most of it. At a time of great expansion in the network, war industries fanned a growing economy, sucking in raw materials and thrusting out war goods. In peace time such cargoes were often transported by sea, but now there was the danger in some coastal areas that they might fall into the hands of the French. Horses were in short supply so that land carriage was even more expensive than usual. The real burden of inland transport fell upon the waterway system and the men at work in it. Their work became increasingly long and arduous and remote from much that a man held dear as distances lengthened and trade pressures increased. The very men who could cope with such work, through experience, were often away in the navy. In short there was a growing shortage of the right kind of hands.

Many captains had to accept such labour as they could get and disreputable characters found their way onto the waterways to taint them for the remainder of their existence. Once the image of the waterways had become tarnished it was ever more difficult, even after the war was over, to recruit decent labour onto the boats. Canal boating was no longer respectable. Sir George Chetwynd reckoned that it was common practice whenever a man lost his character in a neighbourhood for him to say 'I will go and be a boatman'. Speaking of one particularly reprobate youth, a boat master complained, 'we are obliged to employ such Boys as these; we cannot get others'.[20]

There was no shortage of hands after the war; there *was* a dearth of the right kind of labour. In 1873 there was an incident at a flight of locks:

'Crew all full, Cap'n?' a hiccuppy voice inquired as a beery face was thrust through the window of a canal-boat cabin where 'Pop', 'Buffalo Jack' and 'Hansome George' were entertaining William Rideing, a journalist, to breakfast.

'Please God, they aren't half as full as you be!' 'Pop' retorted evasively, at which the 'disagreeable animal slouched away'.

'Congregated in this neighbourhood', Rideing noted regretfully, 'is the rough material of canal life, the tramps and unemployed hands.'[21]

No matter that the unpleasant incident took place upon the Erie Canal in the United States, for such happenings were of daily occurrence in Britain too, especially during the Canal Age. Undesirable elements were said to 'infest the banks of our canals to a very great extent'. Unemployed hands congregated at places like Braunston, Shardlow or Preston Brook, where they lurked 'in beer shops, public houses and bawdy houses', maintaining themselves by poaching and stealing while they waited to be taken on. The hands on the Weaver flats, employed or unemployed, were also 'rather a degraded Class' and were often to be seen 'trespassing about the country' and especially 'on Sunday evening spend their time in practices highly immoral'. The 'purchase men' of Yorkshire were not considered to be a particularly elevated class either.

Nor were captains certain to keep such inferior labour as they had for long. James Hanson, the murderer, showed a marked lack of respect for his captain and the job when among his other insults he shouted: 'Damn thee, I'll murder thee. I don't care a damn for thee or the boat. I can have another tomorrow if I like.'

Often such men or boys disappeared into the night with the captain's shirt or trousers, his flannel coat, even his savings. One boy 'belonging to the Gainsbrough sloop *William*, William Anderson master, laying in Hull harbour, took an opportunity to break open a locker in the vessel, and stole a £10 draft, three guineas in gold and a pair of silver buckles'. Another ungrateful hand, after only a day or two's labour, even stole the horse from his captain, a Skipton boatman.[22] The same shifty itinerant types could still be met with later in the century. George Smith wrote scathingly of one he met in 1878—'a dirty rodney . . . whose whole kit was tied up in a dirty old pocket handkerchief . . .'. Such hands were always leaving the boat for one discreditable reason or another.

Apart from the shortage of the right kind of labour there was also the casual way in which hands were employed, making for a great deal of shifting and changing. A captain, in effect, contracted to haul the boat and its contents from one place to another and he was responsible for all aspects of that haulage. He must provide the lines and horse (this was unusual with a fly-boat but it did happen) and often, especially in the early days, pay for the tolls, tunnel charges and other expenses, as well as providing any labour that he might need to help him. He had to pay such hands and feed them. Some vessel owners did retain the right to make the captain dismiss a man in case of misbehaviour, but he generally had very much of a free hand.

The most common mode of hire was by the voyage (a round trip) or week, but there were many day labourers who could be (and were) paid off almost at a moment's notice. Many of those employed by the voyage or week were equally insecure since they were paid off on the return of the vessel. On the Weaver, for example, the hand was not 'hired if the vessel is standing still— he will go from the Mary Ann to the Jane or the Nancy just as he is wanted', the inference being that if there was no *Emma* or *Sarah* to take him on he must wait unpaid until there was. In bad times he then had to scratch around trying to find some other kind of employment until things improved. There were always casual labourers around the boats who, at the best of times, moved from one job to another.

Life was not always so precarious for the hands. There were those who proved competent and trustworthy. A bond grew up between master and man and they worked together for years on end like James Parcy and William Helsby on the Weaver flat *Wasp* or John Woodhouse and William Butler on a narrow boat working between Tipton and Oxford in 1795. They would pass and repass another permanent team, William Lee and John Linton who always worked the boats of Joseph Dean.

Often there was a family connection of course. Many men worked vessels with their sons or brothers. Thomas Haslehurst worked the flat *Compleat* with his son Jo. Richard Normancy navigated Thomas Russell's coal boat between Tipton and Birmingham with his daughter.[23]

Some Yorkshire vessels were crewed by seven- or three-year 'servants' or apprentices, and on the Old Quay Company's flats also the boy was, from 1814, a regular apprentice, indentured for seven years. He must be ten years of age or above and, like the hand, he worked regularly on the same flat with the same captain.

As elsewhere, the captain was free to appoint his own hand subject to the Company's approval, but there was more security in the sense that such crewmen were the servants of the Company and were not paid by the captain.[24]

The Old Quay Company, as others in Lancashire and Yorkshire, was involved in the carriage of highly valuable commodities and it was particularly interested in finding and keeping decent hands.

As a general rule, however, the 1795 registers reveal that vessels were manned by a named master and 'one man' or 'one boy' (on some of the flats and keels it was a man *and* a boy, on the fly-boats *three* men and a boy), the inference being that it may not have been the same man or boy a week after the register was made up.

Altogether the casualness of canal employment and the fact that there were many young men about, unrestricted by home and community, did mean, especially during the Canal Age, that there were 'goings-on' on the 'cut'. Many of these high-spirited lads grew out of this phase to become honest, respectable and dependable captains. Others did not, some having been really disreputable before they arrived and encouraged to be even more so by the peculiar circumstances of canal life. They either became dishonest and undependable captains or remained a part of the shiftless, shifting mass of canal-boat labour.

It was this fringe element (albeit a substantial one in the early nineteenth century) which was involved in pilfering and other depravities. Many thefts were carried on by bad hands who chose a moment when the master was away to lighten the cargo of their own boat or even another if it was left unattended.

There they were, a 'demoralized' set of men left 'in the centre of a Christian country . . . entirely destitute of all means of moral improvement'.

5
Wind Among the Pines

The difficulty in hiring decent dependable hands was one reason for the emergence of a new development in waterway life—the family boat. The French wars began the problem as young men took up arms or, more likely, were pressed into the navy at a time when the inland waterway's fleet was growing rapidly. As in our own twentieth century wars, women stepped into the breach and with them went their children.

It was on those vessels, working over canals *and* rivers and even the sea—keels, sloops, flats, etc—that women were first to be found. Understandably the hands on these craft would be the first candidates for the navy. In 1802 a coal-laden sloop was upset in the Humber by a sudden gust of wind to reveal on board a woman and two children, one of which, a child of five, perished. Another sloop, loaded with corn, overturned in the canal near Thorne in 1806. Robert Dudding, the master, and his wife managed to escape, but their three children were all drowned.[1] Other tragedies bring to light more women and children on board in the early nineteenth century.

Women probably came onto the narrow boats too during the wars, although there is no hard evidence of their presence until the year after Waterloo when Mary, the wife of John Stamps of Birmingham, was working with him on Pickfords' boat near Banbury.[2] The practice was common enough on the Grand Junction Canal by 1819 when John Hassell, a towpath traveller, remarked that there were 'one or two females generally attending each boat'. By the early 1820s it was commonplace to see women and children passing over the English canals; in 1824 the *Chester Courant*, in describing the canal scene, explained that the boatman's 'wife is on board' as a general observation.

If it were the exigencies of war which brought families onto inland vessels in the first instance, it is clear that something else kept them there and brought others to join them when Napoleon was safely imprisoned on St Helena. It is true that the quality of labour was a continuing, if slowly improving, problem. There were some hard years too in the aftermath of the wars, which brought more women aboard so that captains could make economies. But it was neither poverty nor bad hands which accounted for the large number of families floating over the waterways from the 1820s, for many were not there to replace hired hands. On the Mersey and Weaver flats, for instance, the captain's family was always extra to the crew of three (although the 'boy' was often the master's son). Whatever may have happened during and immediately after the war, by the 1830s the women were not expected to work at the navigation of the vessel even though you might see 'the wife at the helm some-times'.[3] Her job was to look after the men and children and it was generally only at times when all the crew were fully occupied, as in lowering and raising the mast to pass through a bridge, that they might 'make the woman hold on [to the wheel]'.[4]

It was simply the desire for companionship between a man and his family which brought the majority aboard and kept them there. Husbands were away from home for some time and it was natural for wives to prefer to be with them and for the captains to enjoy the comforts of home and family around them. It was the same in other countries with a developed waterway system. 'On all canals', wrote Ethel Springer, an investigator of the American waterways, 'the fact that the inherent nature of the work necessi-tates long periods away from a home on shore is an impelling motive to boatmen to take their wives and children with them.'[5]

Of course, captains were not blind to the economy of taking their dependants with them 'in as much as it is cheaper for a family to live together, the master living perhaps a week from his family', but in general it was not poverty that forced and kept families on board vessels, as has sometimes been suggested. Flat (and keel) masters were prosperous people earning high wages and most of them rented, even owned, houses on shore, where their wives nearly always spent the winter.

Wages were less on the narrow boats, but women were still

often extra to the work of the boat rather than essential to it. Their duties were basically domestic and on many a vessel they merely helped out at certain times, as, for example, when the boats were 'legged' through a tunnel by the men who then 'gave the helm for steerage to the women'. A hand was invariably still employed. In some cases it is understandable why this was so.

Sixteen year old William Winfield acted as 'servant' to William Cox and his wife Nancy in 1851 because they were sixty-four years old, but Charles Sheppard had a wife and six children to help him, one of them a son of fifteen, yet he still employed a twenty-four year old hand, James Knight, in 1871.[6] There were so many boat people like the Sheppards, that it seems fair to conclude that families were not there primarily to work the boat during the Canal Age and even long after. Later they did. As times got harder in the face of railway competition in the later nineteenth century (depending on the type of vessels, people and goods carried) families took an increasingly active role in boating so that by the end of the century they were an essential part of the waterway economy. The women became something of a special breed, as indeed they needed to be to cope with the growing rigours of the life.

'Generally speaking the barge women had a rough life. En voyage they had to steer the barge, prepare the meals and cope with a "tide" of small children', one observer remarked.[7] A

Fig 2 At the tiller, 1884

Government committee of 1921 showed itself to be aware of these trials and tribulations and concluded that,

> ... the living-in conditions on the whole, are not at all ideal for women. The confined quarters of the cabin, the exposure to all kinds of weather, the absence of privacy and the ordinary interests of home life, the discomforts of attending child birth on the boats and the difficulty of giving proper attention to the nurture of young children constitute grave drawbacks to life on canal boats from the point of view of women.

Neither did the NSPCC's Inspector Hackett consider canal boating to be women's work: 'When you see a woman wet half way up to her middle in the winter time and going about half frozen'.[8]

Womankind's natural burden fell more heavily upon the boat women. 'I was born at Braunston', David Hambridge remembered, 'at that white house over there. They were friends of ours and my mother went there off the boats for me to be born.'[9] Other boat women went to friends or to their home on shore if they had one, but many children were born in the cramped cabins—about 50 per cent according to most observers—with all the attendant difficulties. Rarely was a doctor in attendance, or even a midwife before this century, but a 'woman who went about' or the women from nearby boats.

They were remarkably hardy about the whole business. 'They are really in labour when you are sent for', explained one midwife in 1920, 'and the baby is very often born before you get there. They work up till the last hour getting the boat into dock.' In '48 hours you would see them steering the boat again'.[10]

Every one remarked on the ease with which boat women gave birth to children. Deaths and complications were said to be surprisingly few, but no statistics were kept and any damage done through such hasty confinements invariably went unremarked to add to the other burdens which made the stoic boat women old before their time. There are occasional hints of the suffering behind the Amazonian façade. One young boat woman was very distressed when she lost her first baby only a few months old.

'We boat women often get injured through raising lock

Fig 3 Opening the lock, 1884

paddles and working lock gates. I know I shall never be right
again; and I believe that is why my baby did not live. I wish I
could get away from boating, and I think most other boat women
do today.'[11]

Keel work could be equally tough. Harry Fletcher, a keel boy
in the years before World War I, remembered how 'It was a hard
life for a woman. Mother often had to steer the boat if Dad was
busy with other jobs and when there was no wind and no money
to hire a horse, she had to help to haul the keel by hand: strenuous
grinding toil which gave her a strangulated hernia'.[12]

Some boat women at Paddington told George Smith with some
emphasis that the 'boatman who first put a woman into a boat
cabin deserved hanging' and if they had him there they 'would
give him what for—ah! brute! him!'[13] Much depended though
on when and where and by whom they were asked. 'They adore
the life on boats', Mr Childs, a Birmingham inspector, reckoned,
'and then something puts them into a temper and they would be
very pleased to get out of it.' The younger women in particular
were becoming increasingly disillusioned with the life in this
century.

According to the Audlem lock-keeper, on the canals it was the
'weaker sex' that was the stronger one and it was really the
women who, for a century and more, played an important part in
ensuring that heavy bulky goods got through to their destination,
for not only did they have 'their families and barges to steer, but

Plate 7 Mrs Dean and her nephew bow-hauling the keel *Danum* on the Sheffield & South Yorkshire Navigation. Despite the smiles for the camera, bow-hauling was 'strenuous grinding toil' (*Humber Keel and Sloop Preservation Society*)

the grown up children the bargees had to be kept straight when passing through the towns, or when laid up at their journey's end'.[14] The women were the cashiers of the boats 'and very good ones they make, because they hand the money out to the men and they spend it well'. Invariably it was a man's wife who collected his earnings.[15]

The whole business often involved them in 'forceful persuasion and language', and in any trouble they were 'invariably well equipped to retaliate in kind plus bonus'. George Smith, who spent most of his life unearthing unsavoury details of canal life, was less charitable: 'the women are coarse and vulgar, and, if anything can outdo the men in resorting to obscene language and disgusting conversations'. He had

> ... often seen the boat-women strip and fight like men (and if anything more savagely) pulling the hair out of each others' heads by handful, after they had tired themselves by hard hitting with sometimes a little biting into the bargain, to say nothing of kicking.

There were indeed some ''bominable bad uns' among the women-folk too. John Foulstone explained how, when he was bringing the *Susan* into the cut at Doncaster, Hannah Mason, a keelman's wife, stood upon the bridge and hurled stones, dirt and insults down on him. When he got off the vessel she 'got fast hold of his lips and made his mouth bleed very severely'. The chief part of the dispute was carried on with words and ill language and of this the woman 'certainly gave evidence of her amazing powers even before the magistrate making use of some of the most abominable and disgusting language' and it was 'with difficulty that Mrs Mason's tongue could be kept within its proper limits'.[16]

James Loch hinted at other forms of ''bominableness' in a directive concerning the Bridgewater Canal in 1837.

> Sir, I have to request that Directions may be given to enforce Mr Bradshaw's Regulations against Flatmen's and Lightermen's Wives living and sleeping on board with their Husbands. . . . the existence of such a practice, besides affording many excuses for depredation, leads to a system of Morals extremely detrimental and therefore to be avoided.[17]

Fig 4 George Smith (1831–95)

The *Staffordshire Advertiser* was more direct. 'Fornication and adultery are commonly prevalent' the newspaper informed a shocked but interested public in 1840. Conditions were if anything worse by the 1870s according to George Smith who coloured the iniquity with his own particular style of torrential prose.

> The uttermost abomination of immorality, prostitution, impurity and loathsome talk and cursing are to be found. The lewdness, the boldness, the unblushing familiarity, the impudence of gesture, the matter-of-fact falling in with the most profligate indulgences, the open turning aside of mere boys and girls in order to inter-course, the foul songs, the fouler stories, the filthy jokes, the as filthy tricks and the precociousness of the knowledge of things children ought not to know, much less to do, is one of the most terrible elements of the evil training.

Smith reckoned that many boaters had dispensed with the marriage ceremony—over 60 per cent lived 'in sin'—and the crowding together of families and sometimes hands into small cabins led to much immorality. 'Boys and girls of from 12 to 21 years of age are found living together in these floating cupboards', one medical officer of health wrote in disgust. Cases like that of Phoebe Pearsall fanned the sense of public outrage as more and more unsavoury details of canal life were brought to light. It was at the Warwickshire Spring Assizes that

> Phoebe Pearsall and Samuel Pearsall, a mere boy and girl, whose ages were not stated . . . were indicted for having at Chilvers Coton on the 13th September, endeavoured to conceal the body of a child for the purpose of concealing the birth of a female child of the female prisoner.

It was alleged that the girl had given birth to a child in their boat at Griff Colliery and the brother had then thrown the infant into the canal.[18] It was common enough, according to Smith, for such young girls to 'give birth to children, the fathers of which are members of their own family'.

Not everyone agreed with George Smith. Men like John Brydone and Owen Llewellyn, canal boat inspectors, and many others, encountered the same womenfolk. Their descriptions had little in common with those of the earnest reformer. Tom Cubbon has left the most eloquent of these testimonies to another and perhaps truer side of the character of the boat women. Not only were they 'extraordinarily gentle and well mannered', there was also something noble about their looks and bearing. He and his wife

> . . . never—but once—saw a *pretty* face . . . but, what was even more remarkable, they were almost without exception, handsome. The seriousness of life, and the responsibility of their occupation, was shown in every line of their strong features. Long days and nights with Nature, in season and out of season, had marked them for its own. Even their voices had in them a deep, solemn sound, as of wind among the pines.

Their life made them 'thoughtful and self-reliant'. They 'seldom smiled and never laughed' which when they were dressed in their heavy, hooded bonnets gave their 'stern, handsome faces, more the appearance of judges of the High Court than barge-women'. None the less when 'anything went wrong, or anyone was in a fix, there they were, with steadfast eyes looking from under dark brows ready to lend a hand, throw a rope, or lever you off a shallow with a spare tiller'.

Plates 8 *and* 9 Waterway women—they 'seldom smiled and never laughed' and in their heavy hooded bonnets they gave more the 'appearance of judges of the High Court than barge-women'. If rarely pretty 'they were almost without exception handsome': (*above*) narrow-boat family at Berkhamsted on the Grand Junction Canal in the early years of this century (*M. E. Ware*); (*below*) the Theobalds family in the 1920s—Harry, the bishop *manqué* extreme left, his wife extreme right (*the late Harry Theobalds*)

If the nature of the life they led made these women 'thoughtful and self-reliant', such traits were even more necessary when their husbands died or, as often happened, were killed. Brief entries in company minutes such as 'Steerer Stubbs accident and death at Ellesmere Port on 21 May 30 years old—left wife and four children' were all too frequent. Many of these widows struggled on managing the boat alone with their children. In 1877 one barge woman claimed that 'Four out o' six boats as comes from Wigan is worked by women who've lost their 'usbands'.[19] She was probably exaggerating, as boat people were rather prone to do, but the Census returns suggest that the number of women who acted as captains in this way fluctuated between 200 and 600 during the nineteenth century. Janet Smith was one of the Wigan women who, in 1871, was captain of the *Fire King* barge. This thirty-nine year old woman was helped by the three young Booths— Joseph, fourteen, Elizabeth, twelve, and John, five. Widow Mary Bidhurst, sixty, boated iron in the Black Country in the narrow boat *Wrekin* in 1861 with her daughter, twenty, son, seventeen, and grand daughter, twelve.[20] Some of these women owned their own boats. In 1925, for example, 4.2 per cent of the boats inspected passing through Stoke-on-Trent were owned and steered by women.[21]

The burden upon such women and the fortitude and courage with which they faced it can be divined from reading between the lines (whatever the truth of the matter) of a 1935 report on Florence Bentley, aged twelve. She had travelled on a boat going from Northwich to Stoke with her mother, Evelyn Bentley, and brother, fourteen, who drove the horse. There were more children on board. They arrived at Church Locks, Church Lawton at 2.10 am.

> The Coroner (addressing the woman): who attended to them [the locks]?—The boy and myself attended to them. Are they difficult? —Yes.
>
> Why was your daughter, who is only twelve dealing with them this morning?—She was rather frightened of the locks and had been ever since she was four [when the water went into the cabin]. She was a bit nervous and she jumped off the boat while I was attending to the children.
>
> Are you sure she got off unknown to you?—Yes.

Did you make a statement to the police that 'When we arrived at Church Lawton the baby started crying and your daughter said "I will shut the gates for you?" '—No I was frightened then and did not know what I was saying.

What time did the child go to bed?—6 pm.

Did you wake her up?—She woke herself up and got dressed while I was attending to the gates.

Did you permit her to get dressed at two-o'-clock in the morning?—No, she would not go back to bed, but sneaked out after dressing herself.

When did you know she had fallen into the water?—My son shouted out 'mother' thinking I was in the canal. I was in the steering part of the boat which was stationary in the lock. I saw bubbles in the water and picked her up with the hook. I worked on her but it was useless . . . [22]

Different actors had played out a less tragic, if in some ways more poignant, scene in the same heroic story twenty-five years before at Runcorn, amidst Wagnerian weather. 'It was a cold, windy day. A gale swept from one of the widest parts of the Mersey, with the sound of coming snow in it.' A lone woman with a boy of about fifteen and a girl of about twelve were pulling two boats filled with china clay through the locks into the teeth of the gale.

Her clothes were crinkled; the bottom of her skirt was stained with clay and water. Her boots were thin and torn and old. Her face was sad; there was a set sympathetic look in her grey eyes— eyes that seemed to say, 'I know what has been in the past, and what will be before me. I see my life mapped out for me to the end, and I am resigned to it'.[23]

There were never as many boat women as people often claimed —perhaps there might be 3,000 at most in the nineteenth century, reduced to fewer than 1,000 by the 1930s (to be found only in certain regions and in certain types of vessel). None the less they played an important role, greater than their numbers might suggest. Yet as far as the employers were concerned, women crews did not exist. It remained the practice for the boat owner to engage the captain of the boat who, in turn, hired labour to help him. This, in the twentieth century, relieved the boat owner of any responsibility under the various Insurance Acts or the Workmen's Compensation Act so far as the wife and children were concerned. The employer declared that, if anything, they were in the employ of the husband and father. Some boat owners went so far as to pay a woman 5s weekly for keeping the boat clean, but still claimed that she was not in their employ. Hence women (and older children) had no right to claim sickness insurance or compensation in case of injury.

The first step towards a better state of things came in 1924 when two important boat companies, Fellows, Morton & Clayton, and Thomas Clayton (Oldbury), put into operation a scheme by which they were to be responsible for the employment of a captain and a mate on each boat, thereby bringing the women within the National Insurance and Workmen's Compensation legislation. It was not until 1937 that the other large carrier, the Grand Union Canal Carrying Company, seems to have agreed to the same principle. Many women not working for these companies remained outside the schemes.

Plate 10 Unknown boat woman and child at Johnson's Hillock, Leeds & Liverpool Canal. 'I see my life mapped out for me to the end, and I am resigned to it' (*E. Paget-Tomlinson*)

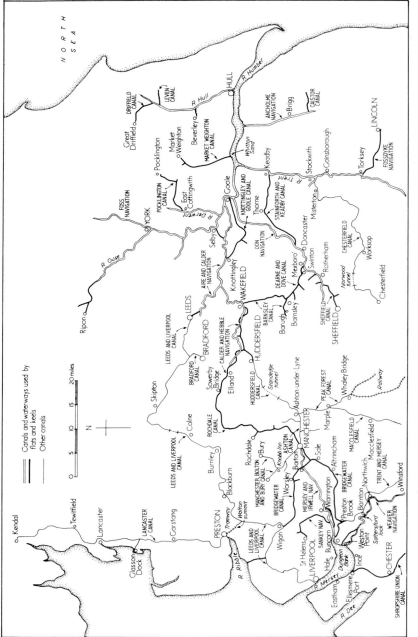

Canals of the North of England

As we have seen, it was not uncommon for a family to hire a boat hand. These were usually boys in their teens, like Robert Brown working on the *Ruth* with George Clark, forty-two and his wife Frances, thirty-three, near Chester in 1871. Sometimes they were younger. James Bunn was nine and his presence as a hand on board the nearby *Rapid* with Thomas (twenty-three) and Harriet (twenty-four) Sadler is explained by the presence of Jessie (two weeks).[24] Sometimes they were older, but this was less usual as such men cost more.

These youths were known as 'chaps'. The position of a chap was a delicate one. Everyone lived crowded together in a narrow stern cabin (occasionally a small fore-cabin was used—more frequently after 1878 and nearly always on the wider vessels). The simple process of going to bed was awkward. According to George Smith the chap

> . . . stood upon the bank while the man, woman, and children were going to bed. After they had settled down, and all was quiet, he crept into the cabin among the children, who lay alongside the father and mother, and in this way all huddled together the whole night.

Such conditions of intimacy could obviously lead to difficulties of temper and temperament. Half a farthing's worth of apples was the cause of one flare up between a chap and his employers in 1878, but there were more deep-rooted tensions at the bottom of it and not least was the fact that four men, one woman and four children were sharing a narrow-boat cabin on a London to Birmingham boat. The apples were a source of dispute between the chap and the children. The mother took their side and a 'stand-up fight' between her and the chap ensued. Her husband, the captain, gave her verbal support. She fought several 'spirited' rounds until 'a severe blow upon one of her eyes somewhat exasperated her' and the 'game' continued with half-bricks and stones. Eventually everyone went into the pub where there was much drinking and exchanging of hard words. An uneasy truce was arranged and the combatants settled down for the night in conditions of ludicrous intimacy.

The next day began well and the Birmingham boat voyaged

Fig 5 A 'chap', 1884

peacefully enough from Rickmansworth to Kings Langley. But passions were simmering and shortly after the boat was the 'scene of a terrible and murderous disturbance'. The captain seized the chap by the throat, threw him to the ground and held him there. He escaped and a free-for-all involving the tiller, stones and other brickbats followed. The chap was nearly pitched into the lock and finally escaped to the *Ouse*, which was 'mating' the Birmingham boat, to travel uneasily with that boat for the remainder of the journey. He had, in any case, been given his 'kit and clearance' after the fight.[25]

Women featured much less in work on the canal banks. There were *some* women lock-keepers, usually carrying on a husband's work at his death if the company would allow them to do so. On the Weaver, for example, when Charles Holland, the Pickering's lock 'tender' died in 1789, he was replaced by his widow, Martha. The faith of the Weaver management in women had remained firm despite a woman lock-keeper at Saltersford, Katherine Boyer, having provoked some difficulty in the previous year by tripping off to Wales leaving a deputy in charge. A sharp note ordering her to return to the lock house proved unavailing and a man replaced her. Women were even appointed in their own right on the Weaver and not infrequently. One woman lock-keeper died in 1801 to be replaced by another as 'Bookkeeper and Lock tender', and there was even at one time a woman blacksmith in the employ of the Trustees.[26] Off the Weaver, women were less favoured, although there was 'Mary Turner, one of the Company's lock keepers', on the Stourbridge Canal in 1830.[27] Only rarely did women feature in other positions. Mrs Hughes succeeded her husband at Pontymoile on the Monmouthshire Canal in 1837 as agent at the same wages,[28] and Mrs Richards was appointed agent and collector at Sandiacre on the Derby Canal at £40 a year in 1866. The appointment was not a success and in 1869 she was given notice, the committee considering that the 'duties cannot be efficiently discharged by a woman'.[29]

Still, there were plenty of women busy ensuring the smooth running of the waterways, but, as on the boats, officially they rarely existed. Wives helped husbands in their work and very often did their work for them when they were away. Mrs Pennington looked after Hargreaves' station at Lancaster in the absence of her husband. One Sunday, when all the family were at church, a man brought a trunk for dispatch to Edinburgh. Mrs Pennington had him put it in the warehouse and then promptly forgot about it. 'Next morning the yardmen were almost driven from the premises by a horrible stench, which they thought came from some hides close by.' It was of course from the trunk that the odour came and it turned out that it had been ejected from the Liverpool–Edinburgh stage-coach 'the passengers protesting that they would "not go one foot further" if that trunk . . . remained on board'. Mr Pennington sent the trunk back to the coach office but, unwanted there, it was left in the street and soon created a sensation. The police eventually opened it and found the bodies of a woman and child crammed inside. It turned out that a Liverpool man had sold his dead (possibly murdered) family to an agent of a medical professor in Edinburgh.

The cottages of the lengthsmen and labourers who worked on canal maintenance in Yorkshire were often situated near swing bridges which were common in that area. At a signal from the fog horn of an approaching keel, the wives of these men would come out to open the bridge, thus performing a useful service since the vessel did not have to stop. As the keel passed, the woman would hold out a long stick with a little bag on the end into which the grateful keelmen would put a penny.[30]

George Smith never looked into the private lives of canal workers on land. He would have found some unsavoury situations if he had—he had a nose for it. The inhabitants of Foxton had petitioned for the removal of Thomas Rathbone from the locks on account of the 'bad character of himself and his family'.[31] Elizabeth Russell of Braunston 'single woman' who on 14 March 1817 'gave birth to a Female bastard child chargeable to the parish of Braunston' charged 'Thomas Walton of Henslow in the county of Oxford clerk to the Oxford Canal Company with having gotten her with child'.[32] At Weston Point one of the Weaver Navigation's employees, John Holford, was said to be keeping 'a disorderly House . . . having three daughters at Home who have five Bastard Children among them'. An investigation was ordered by the disturbed committee and it was true that 'Holford had three Daughters (two of them now at Home the other at service) who had five Bastard Children', but

> Holford himself was a steady inoffensive Character, attending to the Duties of his Situation, but unfortunately [he] had a bad wife of a very loose Character; . . . he had a Lodger, a man in our Employ living in his House who indulged in drunken habits at Holfords, sending for Drink thither, but that as Holford's employment was altogether out of his House, it did not appear such proceedings were with his knowledge.

Poor John Holford—three years later he was dead, drowned on duty at Weston Point.[33]

The canal land workers were not generally considered to be collectively immoral—or dishonest, drunken or dirty (no more were they)—in the way that the boat people were, but their affairs were not pried into so zealously. In fact such people can be found, but then so they can in all walks of life. It is the oldest trick in the world for the eager reformer, as much as for the prejudiced and the evil, to ferret out examples of deviance amongst an unpopular group to tar them all with the same brush—the scrounging unemployed, thieving gypsies, overcrowded orientals are some of the current scapegoats. One wonders if it was not so with the boaters too and that society's prejudices were being hung upon the activities of an unpleasant fringe. So often the accusations were sweeping and general and where specific isolated cases were used in confirmation they did not always, on investigation, match up to the horror expected of them. Phoebe Pearsall and her brother were in fact acquitted and so were the men accused of raping Elizabeth Clayton, though there is little doubt that they had made improper approaches to her. Even in that worst affair of all—the Christina Collins case—though the men were found guilty, there remains some doubt as to whether she was murdered, committed suicide or was accidentally drowned. It is questionable whether the boatmen really had a fair trial.

The waterway folk were perhaps not always quite what the public thought them to be. Certainly as far as women were concerned there were many in a position to know who reckoned that the presence of wives on board, in both Britain and America, kept them steadier and generally raised the moral tone of the waterways rather than lowered it. There was much about waterway life that was misunderstood and not least the job itself.

6

Nobody seems to be doing anything like Hard Work

The canals were the wonder of the eighteenth century, exciting and enjoying awe. In the growing bustle of the nineteenth century they were increasingly ill at ease. Admiration turned to impatience and then to derision. 'No important improvement has been made since their original formation,' Thomas Townshend railed in 1846. 'Generally speaking they are mere ditches of endless sinuosity . . . nothing has aroused the Canal Companies from the torpitude which they have not the resolution to shake off.'[1]

When the brash *nouveaux riches* railways steamed much of the bustle away one senses almost a feeling of relief in the canal world that they could now return, a little hurt and shaken perhaps—but as gentlemen of course—to the eighteenth-century way of life that they understood and which they had, for the most part, left with reluctance. It was very much as eighteenth-century institutions that the canals wandered down into the twentieth century. 'If it were necessary to select that kind of business in which absolutely neither enterprise nor inventive faculty have ever come into play and to award a medal for that distinction, it may be asserted with safety that canals would receive the medal', 'Hercules' wrote scathingly in 1885.[2]

In October 1923 the humble *Record* complained 'They are fifty years behind the times'; longer according to the mightier *Times* which chided: 'Canal companies have with a few exceptions been "sitting on the fence" for the last 100 years'; and worse, they had for the most part 'sunk into desuetude'.[3] By then the canals were on the verge of becoming 'quaint', ensuring their survival into yet another century.

It was all very leisurely. The system of tolls and carriage rates charged to canal users was not only discouragingly complex and haphazard, but left much to the initiative of the many rare characters who found employment on the canals. On the Lancaster Canal there was an early form of decision sharing.

When Myles Pennington arrived at Preston as a new clerk, his first job was to 'charge out' the way-bill on some goods in from Manchester.

'Where are the rates?' he asked of the agent.

'Oh, call in Joe, he knows more about rates.'

Joe Hornby, the carter who collected and delivered goods in Preston, 'a clean-shaven rather pleasant looking fellow', came into the office and the process of 'charging out' began. Joe 'strokes his hair in front and looks wondrous wise'.

'Tommy Careful, one bale?' queries Pennington.

'Fourteen pence,' says Joe.

'Billy Sharp, one bale.'

'He'll only stand one shilling.'

'Peter Careless, one truss.'

'He'll stand eighteen pence.'

And so it went on, people paying different rates for the same type of goods from the same place according to what a man, in Joe's estimation *could stand*. It was a progressive even socialist system; esquires, reverends, military officers and the nobility paying according to their station in life.

The system was equally democratic on the Old Grand Union. Directives went out from the management committee, but they were 'in numberless instances set at nought and neglected by the Toll Collectors, who appear to have adopted almost as many systems as there are traders on the Canal'. Supervision was easy-going since 'a very great laxity existed with reference to the mode in which the Accounts of the Toll Collectors were checked'.[4]

A few concerns were perhaps more efficiently and energetically managed, especially where they had a regular and substantial trade—the Aire & Calder, the Weaver, the Sharpness New Docks Company, the Birmingham Canal Navigations and the Grand Junction—but the events of 1874 showed that there were weaknesses in the day-to-day management of even the largest companies. Henry Gawthorne complained to the *Times* on 8 October of the Grand Junction Company's laxity in handling

Fig 6 Regent's canal explosion, 2 October 1874

and storing gunpowder at the Paddington Wharf. It was

> . . . deposited in a shed or open warehouse with various other
> goods, without any special precaution for the prevention of
> accident—for into this place men have been seen to enter with a
> naked light, apparently heedless of the fearful danger they
> incurred—until a boat is ready to receive it. It is then put into a boat
> with other miscellaneous cargo, and that in the most careless

manner. A fire is generally burning in these boats, and has been observed while the powder has been loading into the vessel. I have myself seen a ton or thereabouts of powder in uncovered barrels in the open warehouse and a naked jet burning within 3ft of it. . . .

The local sanitary inspector, he added, had seen a man climbing over a boat loaded with gunpowder, a lighted pipe in his mouth. Others confirmed that there were not only fires and smoking boatmen on the Grand Junction Company's powder boats, they were often loaded with benzoline and other highly inflammable materials at the same time. The information all came too late. On 2 October 1874 one of these boats blew up on the Regent's Canal with the loss of several lives and considerable damage to property.

The whole set up had much of the eighteenth century about it in pace and organisation. Canal boating seemed to be just as leisurely. In 1921, for example, Sydney Preston grumbled about the attitude of the canal workers (or the trade unions) and the 8-hour day. At Hampstead, he explained, there was a series of locks, and in the early morning it was a regular occurrence for from sixteen to twenty boats to be waiting to pass through. As one barge occupied 15 minutes in negotiating these locks, 5 hours were so occupied by the twenty barges collected overnight. Thus the man in charge of the last barge had put in 5 hours' 'duty' before doing anything. As the principle of the 8-hour day had been extended to canal employees (including the Regent's Canal bargemen), this man had only 3 hours' more work to perform before he tied up his barge again.[5]

Nor did the work seem particularly exhausting when the boats were on the move. It involved steering the boat, driving the horse, negotiating the locks and sometimes loading and unloading. Steering was not very exacting, according to 'Hercules'. 'The steersman is blowing white puffs from a short pipe, setting up a line of thin smoke in competition to that arising from the small funnel of the cabin stove. . . . Now and then the boatman breaks out into snatches of song. . . .' Driving the horse was even more relaxing, not to say somnolent:

The horse mostly has a driver, who, being mounted on the steed's back, occasionally lies there at full length, ending in falling asleep. The horse discovering this goes slower. . . . When horse and boy both go to sleep, however, and come to a standstill, it is awkward because the boat's draught prevents its being taken near enough to the land to enable the boatman to jump ashore and take active measures to induce a movement onward, and he is reduced to hurling such missiles as the cargo of the boat may provide at the offenders to stir them up.

'Nobody', added 'Hercules', 'seems to be doing anything like hard work.'

There was a reason for this somnolence, however, and it was not because of the relaxed nature of canal boating. In fact Sydney Preston's complaint was an oblique admission of the many extra hours' work that boatmen had put in to make up lost time. By general testimony the hours were long and awkward. And if some of those hours were spent in waiting around at locks, wharfs and tunnels it was still part of the job. No one accuses a lorry driver of not working when he is caught in a traffic jam.

In the 1840s John Hollins tried to persuade some boatmen to come to church one evening.

'We are too tired, sir,' they complained with sincerity. 'We've been at work since half-past two (in the morning . . .) and we are going to have tea and turn in.'

Nor was it an unusual day for, in 1877, the reporter of the *Standard* explained 'On long journeys the periods of rest or "tying up" are made as brief as possible and may be reckoned at about seven out of the twenty-four hours—or from eight in the evening until three the next morning'. Edward Lloyd, manager of the Warwick canals, confirmed to the *Select Committee on Canals* of 1883 that 'they generally travel 16 hours out of 24' at '30 miles a day'. In Britain, on the continents of Europe and America the story was the same—fifteen hours was the very minimum working day. So it continued until the 1960s. Rose and Jack Skinner working a Willow Wren pair in the twilight years of narrow boating would be up with their family at five and work non-stop until eight or nine at night with essential chores extending Rose's working day to eleven or twelve. 'It's not much sleep,' she admitted, 'but you get used to it.'

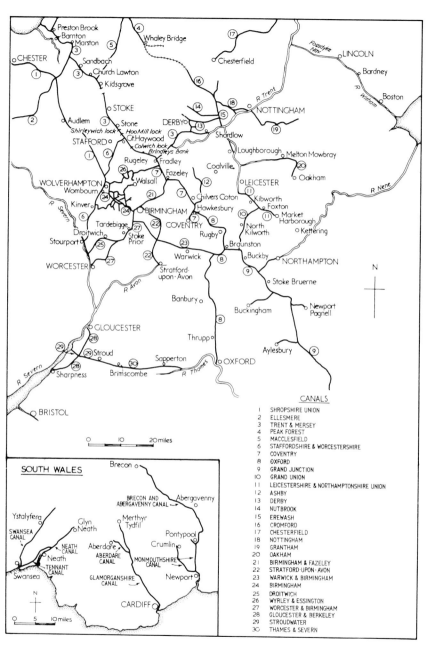

Canals of the Midlands and South Wales

89

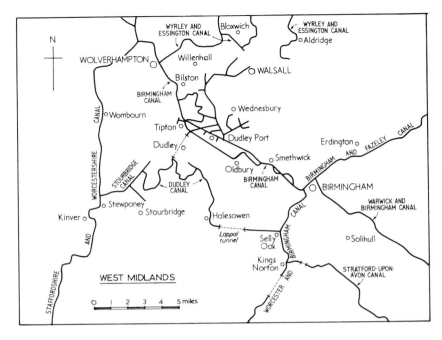

Canals of the West Midlands

In addition there were exceptional circumstances; an important cargo to be delivered or a rush of trade—a 'throng' was how the flatmen described it. One of the Gloucester boatmen explained to Hollins how, a short time before, they had been so 'hurried on' that for a fortnight they worked night and day and the horse never saw the inside of a stable.

'We kept him going by putting plenty into him.'

There was no rest at the weekend either. The English canal boatmen 'groaned beneath the yoke of Sunday work'.

'I was in one boat for six years', another boatman told Hollins, 'and had but three or four Sundays free from work.'

The Sabbath, once so religiously observed in the early days of the canals, had become, by the 1820s, a working day like any other for many canal workers. It was the same in the USA. Captain Parkhurst, who refused to work on a Sunday, was so unique that his craft was known everywhere as 'the Sunday boat'. Intermittent agitation arose on both sides of the Atlantic to abate

Sunday working, until the Christina Collin's case, in coinciding with tractarianism and a general religious revival, did bring about some reduction in Sunday working in Britain. Not so in the USA—the Delaware & Hudson was the only canal that strictly kept the Sabbath holy in America.[6]

'We don't know it's Sunday', said one American boatman in 1922, 'till we see some folks along the way, dressed up and a-goin' to Sunday school.'

Working conditions were at their worst on the fly-boats—express vessels travelling non-stop night and day using relays of horses to maintain an average speed of about 3 mph. It was a peculiar sort of job—snatched sleeps in cramped, often noisy, conditions, snatched meals and snatched pleasures at the end of the trip, before the next began within a few hours of arrival—to Birmingham, Manchester or London many miles and days away. Not surprisingly 'young rollicking fellows' usually took on the job, like the men on Mr Essex's fly-boat whose 'rollickings' (or attempted rollickings) with Elizabeth Clayton made news in 1823.

'We are worse off than slaves,' the English watermen concluded dolefully, 'for they never knew what liberty was, but we are slaves in a free country.'

Altogether it is hardly very surprising that everyone was beginning to nod off after sixteen hours, and more, on the go. Joe, the hand of the *Mary Jane*, snatched every minute of sleep that he could and when working on ahead preparing the locks was invariably 'found dead asleep on his ordinary bed, the gangway of a lock gate'.[7]

Even the lightest activity carried on for sixteen hours becomes burdensome and the steering of a loaded horse boat was not in fact particularly light work. Steering a barge was 'as energetic as tennis in a fast doubles'. The steerer had to stand up all the time and the task needed a surprising amount of concentration and skill. Driving the horse was equally tiring. Thomas Hales, manager of the Shropshire Union Company, reckoned that few drivers in practice rode on the horse's back, but plodded increasingly wearily in its wake. It was particularly unpleasant and tiring in wet weather when the towpath became muddy and slippery, for the work went on. 'It never rains, snows or blows for a boatman,' said one. More and more verbal (and physical) encouragement was needed as the animal flagged.

In fact, few of the boaters would stand at the helm or walk behind the horse (excluding passage through locks and tunnels) for a full 16-hour day, although it did happen. In the early days of the canals, when journeys were short, a boy or man was specifically hired to 'drive the horse'. Gradually a code of work evolved and one person would be driving only for 'two or three hours at the most at one time. They give them "spell and spell about" as they term it'. The canal system was divided into work zones by the boat people usually beginning and ending with a bridge known as a change bridge (not to be confused with 'change line' or 'turnover' bridges where the towpath (and horse) crossed from one canal bank to the other). One of these bridges was the Half-Way Bridge $4\frac{1}{2}$ miles down the Shropshire Union Canal from Ellesmere Port. Here the person who began driving at the port got onto the boat, and some one else took his place. They were 'constantly changing about'. The fly-boats worked on a similar system. They did not have two of the crew working by day and the other two by night, but changed over after four miles or so. The driver came to steer, the steerer went to rest and one of the off duty men went to drive. The length of duty and of rest was about eight miles or four hours, but there was a change round every two hours.[8]

On European and American waterways it was more common for men to be hired specifically to drive and the driving spells were longer. In the USA, unless there was a large family aboard able to do its own driving, there were usually two drivers to a boat working six hours a day and six hours a night, each man's animals changing with him to return to the stable at the front of the boat. Night driving was the worst—'All alone in the dark', complained one driver, 'and no one to talk to 'cept a mule, it's mighty lonesome. Then when it rains an' is stormy it's not much fun peggin' along an' hollerin' at your mule.' He would dream of the time when he might become a steerer or while away the time with observation of the mules' ears—if he could see them.

Something cur'us about them mules. You can ca'c'late their age pretty close every time by the way they wobble their ears. Take a young mule, and he twists 'em all shapes all the time; when he gets old he quiets down and holds 'em kinder steady. They're mighty good for telling the weather, too; when a mule keeps his ears pricked up its a sure sign of rain.[9]

In Britain horses were more common than mules and many became sufficiently well trained to go by themselves.

If they are not coming to any locks and they have a quiet part of the canal to go through, the horse goes along by itself; there is only the person steering . . . the horse is trained to do so; and if the steerer sees another boat coming he turns the boat to the shore, and a person gets off to pass them; a very large amount of mileage is worked in that way without anybody driving at all.[10]

If the horse refused to fall in with these arrangements—and the burden of a 16-hour day fell no where more heavily than upon this long-suffering animal—there was always the 'lazy driver'; a clog or tin can tied to the horse's tail to make him believe that someone was close on his heels.

Some boatmen curried favour with their horses.

' "Keep her belly full", says I to Joe, "keep her belly always full Joe, and then 'er goes 'long like a steam ingin," ' Captain Jonah explained.

Failing the carrot there was always the stick which usually came in the form of a huge whip. There was also the verbal stick. 'Loving words—though of a sanguinary nature almost invariably beginning with a big big B— are freely used. . . . The flexibility of these words, and the wonderful power of modulation acquired by the bargee, usually gives them full command over the horses, who know to a nicety how far they may take advantage of the humours of the drivers'. For there was something of an art in driving, as the reporter of the *Standard* found when he tried it, leaving a trail of havoc down the canal in the process.

''Er's a darned sight too cunnin' for yer guvnor,' Captain Jonah told him. ''Er's dreadful cunnin' if 'er once catches sight that it ain't Joe as is walkin' after 'er. . . . You should never let that 'ere 'orse see yer. Keep behind 'er I always says to Ellen, and then there's no stoppin' the boat.'

The whip had two, possibly three, functions. The crack which

Plates 11, 12 and 13 Canal horses: (*above*) the horse takes a well earned rest at Northchurch, Dudswell, on the (new) Grand Union Canal, August 1935. Note the inevitable feeding bowl. Many a horse worked extremely long hours and they 'kept him going by putting plenty into him' (*Hertfordshire County Records Office*);

the long lash made at the hands of a proud boater served as a warning to the steerers of oncoming boats, and to the driver's own steerer, that danger (one crack) was near. Three cracks meant that all was well as a boat approached a bridge hole or some other hazard. The sound from the straightening lash served as another incentive to a flagging horse, but it was only the crack according to the Cubbons who 'never during our month among them did we see a whip used on the back of a horse'. Many an animal might have told a different tale. If it was not whipping it was some other form of torture for there is no doubt that many boat horses were badly treated if only in the sense that they toiled for such long hours. They might have fared better had they been of any sort of quality before they came on to the canal, but there were a lot of 'thirty shilling horses', which could be got for pulling boats when nobody else would buy them. There was 'not much spirit or kick in them'. For the most part they were 'broken down cab horses', though there were rejects of all kinds and not a few stolen horses found their way onto the canals. Some were

(*below left*) A 'thirty-shilling horse' with the family that worked him over the Trent & Mersey Canal, 1909. Many were rejected cab horses and were badly treated (*Director, NSPCC*); (*below*) Jim Hollingshead's horse at Acton Bridge on the same waterway '*Some* boatmen took great pride in their animals . . .' (*Mrs Agnes Hollingshead*)

blind. Barges, flats and keels were pulled by larger beasts, but they found the work equally hard. 'The horses had a poor time of it,' wrote Harry Fletcher, 'and had a shorter life than most for keel hauling was a killing job. They were worked until their strength failed, then were sold to horse dealers and put down to end up as dog-food, fats and bone meal. I never heard of any being put out to grass or given honourable retirement.'

The horses were always tired and the boatmen were always in a hurry. There was much ill treatment from man to beast in attempts to reconcile incompatible aims in the minds of each. In America, too, animals were 'dreadfully abused' and 'either from the nature of the duties imposed or from bad treatment, exhibit the most disgusting spectacles'.[11] One horse working on the Bridgewater Canal was found to have an off shoulder that was a mass of sloughing sores from top to bottom, two ulcerated wounds, one on each side of the chine, old wounds on the off hind and near fore legs and to be in an impoverished condition—totally unfit for work.[12]

Sore shoulders was the main occupational complaint suffered by these animals. The temptations for a boatman, dependent upon the horse for his living, to carry on when a respite was essential are obvious and many did. Another common affliction was a dislocated shoulder. A ducking in the canal was the usual form of treatment, the idea being that in the struggle to get out the shoulder would go back. It was something of a 'kill or cure' solution.

Falling into the canal was another occupational hazard. Horses

Fig 7 A heavy load

often missed their footing, got caught up in the ropes or were pulled into the water when a boat went unexpectedly off course in an accident as when

> ... the Horse belonging to the Steerer of the Boat 'Dorothy' was pulled into the Canal between Chester and Ellesmere Port owing to the rope attached to the Boat being caught under the Boat 'Arcturius' passing in the opposite direction. The horse was injured and died a few days afterwards. ...[13]

Many horses met their deaths in this way.

Mules were often preferred because they were more sure-footed than horses. They were less popular in Britain except on the Worcester & Birmingham and Bridgewater canals, but were widely used in Europe and America probably also for the reason given by an American driver.

'A mule kin stand it better 'n a hoss. Take a hoss and it only takes a few seasons to wear him out. Now you mayn't believe it, but that off mule has been pulling a boat twenty-three years.'

They were more difficult to drive, however. 'Wal, yes; they git kinder rumbunctious sometimes,' he admitted.

There was greater cruelty in the early days just as there was elsewhere until the public conscience became more concerned with the welfare of animals. Increasing numbers of horses came to be supplied by the large carrying companies and they looked after them very well, fining and dismissing any boatmen who mistreated them. *Some* boatmen took great pride in their animals and cared for them as best they could, but they remained in the minority and though much of the cruelty was thoughtless rather than intentional, it was no fun to be a boat horse.

There was time to catch up on lost sleep for both horse and men at the end of the journey. 'There is a good deal of delay in the daytime in attending to the boat at the wharves when taking in and landing cargo, and one of the men would have rest whilst they are discharging and loading,' Thomas Hales explained. It was by no means always the rule for boatmen to load and unload their boats, especially during the Canal Age and especially if they worked for large companies. The Shropshire Union boats were generally 'dealt with by the wharfingers and servants'.[14]

Plates 14, 15 and 16 Canal staff: (*above*) maintenance men at work with the spoon dredger *Oregon* on the Trent & Mersey Canal *c* 1906 (*the late Enoch Appleton*); (*below left*) a lock-keeper and his wife *c* 1900 (*M. D. Bennet*); (*below right*) new lock gates being fixed by craftsmen and others, probably on a Grand Junction lock *c* 1908 (*Waterways Museum*)

Unfortunately some time elapsed from starting out to journey's end. An average slow boat voyage from Runcorn to London was said to take eight to nine days at 30 miles a day in 1883; from Wolverhampton to London about a week. Fly-boats took about three days from Birmingham to London and about five days from Manchester to London until steam and then motor boats speeded up times. In 1923 steam-towed boats made the Birmingham trip 'at the giddy speed of forty-eight hours' travelling night and day. But for most boatmen sleep was an item snatched rather than taken.

The lock-keepers and lengthsmen were basically watchmen who guarded against the ravages of time, nature and especially boatmen acting to the detriment of the workings of the canal. The lengthsman patrolled a section of canal, observing the feeders and overflow weirs, inspecting the aqueducts and banks, especially at embankments, for any sign of damage or weakening giving prompt notice of any repairs needed. The lock-keeper kept his lock in decent order, perhaps carrying out some repairs himself. In addition he would usually help boats through, whether he was obliged to or not, though this was not his main function as a general rule—to prevent the 'depredations' of the hurrying boatmen was why he was there.

It was not an unpleasant occupation. He lived by his work usually in pleasant surroundings and he often had time to tend his garden and pass the time of day. On the quieter canals the company might help to fill his time by expecting him to double as carpenter, reservoir man, pump minder, toll-collector, or even in one instance as wharfinger. Sometimes they were asked to keep an eye open for drunken boatmen, for signs of pilfering, for evidence of cheating the toll-collector.

Labourers and craftsmen were always at work in maintaining the canal under the orders of the length foreman or ganger who in turn was under the orders of the engineer. They worked on repairs that the lengthsmen had spotted needed doing, on lock work beyond a keeper's capabilities, on a bridge, in a tunnel (usually at night), on piling a weak spot in the bank. Dredging, using the laborious manual spoon dredger (more recently replaced by the steam dredger), went on all through the year. Major repairs could only be carried out by closing the canal and such

Plates 17 and 18 Labourers on the Grand Junction: (*above*) preparing for the building of a retaining wall on the Buckingham Arm on a cold grey day during the stoppage of 1913 (*Waterways Museum*); (*below*) preparing the floor of a lock for concreting, 1925 (*Waterways Museum*). Both photographs show the unpleasant conditions under which labourers worked

jobs were reserved for the annual stoppage of a week or so, usually in May or June. Preparations went on through the winter months at the company's maintenance depots. Lock gates were made by the carpenters, stone work prepared by the masons, paddle gear by the blacksmiths. Then it was all hands to the pumps as the jobs were completed, the men working long hours often in bad weather in slimy lock chambers or dank tunnels always in a hurry to get the work finished so that traffic could start again. Extra labourers would be hired to clean out the empty pounds or a tunnel of mud and debris.

Apart from toll-collectors, who examined boat permits, gauged vessels to check the weight of the load and collected tolls, the rest of the land staff would be found at wharfs. There were the public wharfs of the canal company and the private wharfs of such traders as Pickfords, Crowley & Hicklin, Bache & Co, and so on. They all worked on the same principle. An agent was, among other things, in charge of several wharfs. Each wharf was under the direction of a wharfinger, who was responsible for all the activity at these 'stations'.

His was perhaps the most 'public' of all the canal jobs in the sense that he was in the firing line from the most number of people—from irate customers complaining of damaged, delayed or pilfered goods, to frustrated boatmen fighting to load or unload, perhaps blocking the main line of the canal in the process. This was the most difficult of Mr Hipkiss' tasks in the early years of the Birmingham Canal until facilities came nearer to meeting the demands upon them. 'Great complaints' had been made to the committee 'of the Willfull disobeyance of the Company's Bye laws at the Wharf', and Hipkiss was given orders to deal firmly with the offenders. His successor still had to cope with 'great disorders' at the wharf.[15]

Some of the responsibility for the security of the goods was delegated to a warehouseman although the wharfinger had the final responsibility. Porters loaded and unloaded the boats watched by check clerks backed up by invoice clerks perhaps under the control of a shipping clerk depending upon the size of the wharf. At the smaller stations the wharfinger might do everything himself. At the main wharf there would often be even more clerks working in the head office of the canal company as at

Plate 19 Stewponey Wharf on the Staffordshire & Worcestershire Canal. Carters, wharfmen and boaters pause for the camera *c* 1905. Congestion sometimes led to conflict. A wharfinger—possibly the man with the watch and handkerchief—had charge of a wharf (*M. E. Ware*)

Plate 20 Unloading (and loading) remained primitive and largely manual until recent times: unloading coal in Liverpool. The work got harder as the boat was emptied (*Liverpool Corporation, City Engineers Dept*)

the Crescent Wharf, Birmingham. There would be copy clerks, clerks working on toll negotiations and 'drawbacks', confidential clerks, book-keepers—all working to the orders of the man who made the company tick (or otherwise) variously known as the manager, secretary, agent, superintendent or clerk.

The hours were long by present standards. Twelve hours was a minimum for most canal workers in the eighteenth and nineteenth centuries. The work of a lock-keeper, for example, was not unduly taxing, but even in the early days, when the canals were closed at night, eighteen hours might pass in summer before he could again fix the chain and padlock that guaranteed his rest. The wharfinger who was expected to be at his post on the Brecon Wharf from 4 am to 10 pm in the summer would not be untypical.[16]

Even the lock and chain could not ensure complete repose as the fly-boats began to arrive from the 1790s with their night licences. The Trent lock-keeper on the Erewash Canal complained that he was much troubled in the night by having to get up to let boats through. He was allowed to charge 1s to each boat that disturbed his rest, 2s on Sunday.[17] Sometimes they hired an assistant with the extra money. More often their wives handled the job for a time during the day while they caught upon their sleep. Wharfingers suffered from the same encroachment into uncivilised hours—'in case of need, the wharfinger shall stop up at Nights to render every facility for the despatch of all Vessels which are under necessity of sailing during the night', the Rochdale Company ordered in February 1824.

The more important canals were open night and day and Sundays by the 1830s and at the busiest points men worked shifts. Otherwise many a lock-keeper retired to bed and left the boatmen to it, but the responsibility was always there and he slept with one ear open. Lengthsmen too must be for ever vigilant even when their day's work was done. It was exactly when a man might most welcome the comfort of his cottage on a wet stormy night that he must be about checking the levels and the banks for fear of flooding and breaches, perhaps carrying out hasty measures himself in the loneliness of the night before alerting others to danger. For the most part they were loyal and dedicated men who would think nothing of walking many miles in heavy rain to

open an overflow sluice. So too were the labourers and craftsmen who would be called out to any emergency to work long hours, day and night and at the weekend, in tough weather conditions, and with the threat of danger there all the time.

The job of the flatmen and keelmen was somewhat different from that of their inland brethren. They were canal boatmen part of the time and sailors the rest. Their vessels were different too. They were about twice as wide as the traditional narrow canal boats and were built to pass upon estuarial and even coastal waters, being fitted with a single mast rising to about 50ft above the water. Under favourable conditions this mast could be lowered in about fifteen minutes to pass under low bridges, but it took almost twice as long to raise it again. Hence the mast was usually struck completely and removed from the vessel on entering the inland waterways proper, although captains sometimes made use of a favourable wind wherever the bridges were few and far between, especially in Yorkshire where there were long straight stretches and swing bridges.

In the early days of the Mersey & Irwell Navigation men had pulled the flats and on the Weaver men acted as haulers until 1840. This was a job that they then gave up to the horse with some reluctance, not very surprisingly since, being forced out of work, many had to 'get among the stones jobbing where they can'. According to Mr Hostage, the solicitor to the Weaver Trustees, 'there was a strong resistance to it and I was directed to indict some of the parties'.[18]

Plates 21 *and* 22 Repair work on the Grand Junction: (*above*) extensive repairs to three locks began at 4 am on Sunday 13 June 1909. This picture shows work in progress at lock 97. The work was completed by 7.30 pm and boats passed again from early Monday morning (*Waterways Museum*); (*below*) at 2 pm on Sunday 20 December 1914 the weir at lock 99 was blown away by flood water. Canal company officials feared it would take six weeks to get traffic going again. R. S. Tuvell, London District Overseer (in the bowler hat), had his men working night and day. Traffic was resumed on Christmas Day at 4.30 am after four and a half days (*Waterways Museum*)

The system of hauling flats and keels came nearer that in Europe and America. At certain points along the waterway men waited with their horses to be hired for a specific distance—'horse marines' they were called in Yorkshire. They were not members of the crew. Their whole day—and night sometimes—was spent with the horse. The haulers on the Weaver were considered to be the lowest form of waterway life in the 1840s and as late as 1875 the Reverend Bell, Vicar of Goole, complained to the Factory Commission 'The class of men that give us the most trouble on canals are the men that drive the horses, the hauling men'.

Once they left the relative calm of the canals and navigations the flatmen and keelmen needed different skills; those concerned with sails, masts and the helm, the wind, the tide and above all the 'deeps'. In such estuaries as the Mersey and Humber there were tricky passages to be sought out between sand banks deceptively covered by the tide and which often, according to one master, 'gradually shift every spring tide'.

Knowledge and constant soundings were necessary to avoid running on the banks for 'when you are navigating the river in a dark night you cannot always avoid it', especially at such tricky spots as just below Runcorn where the Mersey narrowed sharply and entered upon a circuitous course, intersected by sand banks and by marshland projecting from the banks. The Dungeon Bank in the Mersey and the Whitton Sand in the Humber were treated with particular respect.

It is a credtt to the skill of the flatmen and keelmen that they in fact rarely ran aground though sometimes

The circumstances of persons occasionally getting neaped [aground for one or several tides] upon the sand banks principally arises from the negligence in not attending to their soundings, or the temerity or rashness in standing too near the banks.[19]

And rough weather could take even the most skilled unawares.

7
More Dangerous than the Sea

In 1928 a reporter of the *Sheffield Independent* watched the keel *Hope* swing into view on the last stage of her journey from the Humber.

> Into a spectacle of smeared greys and gloomy blacks the barge brought a splash of colour—a blue marked water line and gay painting round the aft cabin . . . her skipper singing at the tiller and a cheerful wisp of blue smoke curling up from her stubby funnel . . . a gentle-eyed Labrador, sat steadily by the tiller.

When she had docked he peeped into the cabin where 'everything was clean and the cabin lamp flooded the place with a warm glow'.

'You've a nice place,' he told the keelman.

'They are not always so,' rejoined the captain sadly and he explained how years before he had lost his mother, wife and three sisters in a river mishap where the victims were imprisoned in their cabin when the vessel capsized.

For the keelmen and flatmen, as for anyone moving or working in such raw natural elements as wind and tide, there was a greater degree of risk than for most landed occupations. Sometimes whole crews would go down with their vessels. These men were not foolhardy. Always they worked warily with the elements. But the estuarial waters of the Mersey and the Humber could become 'grey and savage' almost in a matter of minutes. In 1825 for instance there was a night of destruction and tragedy on the Mersey when two flats were lost and others thrown aground or in difficulty. The Old Quay Company's *Fox*, laden with corn for Manchester, was 'upset' on the Dungeon Bank in the gale and the crew of three perished. Another flat belonging to the Bridgewater Trustees was sunk in the 'deep' of the middle passage between Hale and Ince and her crew seems to have been lost. Several other vessels were driven on shore by Ince.[1]

On the longer, more open estuary of the Humber, with no Ireland or Wales to temper the winds suddenly scything in from the North Sea, there was even greater danger. Of all the tragedies played out there the most poignant was in 1808 when

> ... a trader from Leeds to Hull, Vessey, Master, in going down with a cargo of coals was stranded below Witten Sands: at the time the vessel foundered, the master, his pregnant wife and two of their children were on board. His first care was to save his wife; whom he carried in his arms from the vessel to the shore, a distance of about a mile; he immediately returned to his children, and notwithstanding the rapidity of the current and the interruption of the large sheets of floating ice, he succeeded in getting them on shore, when awful to relate he found his wife a corpse, and to complete the climax of heart rending distress, his two children, overcome by intense cold expired in his arms.[2]

Mortality from accidents among British inland watermen in the nineteenth century was appallingly high and during one period it was even higher than that for seamen. This was long after steam tugs with their greater speed and manoeuvreability had done much to reduce dangers in estuarial waters. As early as the 1830s, after some failures in the 1820s, the supremacy of steam tugs over sails was widely accepted. 'They expedite business much quicker and better and with far greater safety,' John Askew, the Liverpool harbour master, commented in 1838.[3]

In the second half of the nineteenth century sails quickly disappeared from the Mersey and the Weaver—although there were survivals into the twentieth century. More and more goods came to be carried in dumb barges. The job that had once demanded the skill and iniative of a master craftsman, rewarded by a considerable degree of independence, was for many flatmen reduced to one of nudging an unrigged vessel into obedient line with others behind the steam tug in a brief passage over the Mersey. Sails disappeared from the Humber too, but sails and rigging were kept because keelmen could often use the wind inland. In hard times the waters of the Humber would come alive again as keelmen who could not afford the tug beat hopefully towards the good cargo in Hull that would set them straight again.

There were still dangers and men continued to die in estuarial waters, but the risks were much reduced with the coming of steam. The changing modes of operation also greatly reduced the number of families aboard flats if not keels. It was relatively rarely that one found women and children aboard Mersey flats by the late nineteenth century.

None the less deaths from accidents for all watermen were still very high at the end of the nineteenth century. It may be quite wrong to look for the causes where one would most expect to find them, that is upon rivers and estuarial water rather than upon calm inland canals, for there is a distinct impression that it was exactly here that the men (and women and children) were being killed. Certainly canal boating was far from being the carefree pursuit that it appeared.

There was one task in particular that played a significant part in the death toll, and which for many years there was no way round; no 'lazy driver' to fall back on. This was the job of getting the boats through the tunnels. There were no towpaths through most of them. Boats had to be 'legged' through until late in the nineteenth century when steam or electric tugs were introduced at many tunnels.

Fig 8 Legging

One lucky member of the crew led the horse overland. The others pushed the boat into the tunnel with the boat hook. Then the boatmen, and sometimes the women, would lie on their backs across the front of the boat and placing their feet on the slippery side walls would by a side stepping motion begin to inch their way through the 'wet brown intestine into the very bowels of the earth'. It was a laborious task which could drag on as long as three hours in dank dark surroundings. It demanded 'all the strength, patience and judgement that the boatmen can command'. In the wider tunnels two planks called 'wings' were fixed to the front of the boat, upon which the men would lie in order to bring their feet within reach of the walls.

Usually only one of the men from the boat 'legged' through any one tunnel; the other side would be propelled by a professional 'legger' who would wait with his 'wing' by the black mouth of his work place. For much of the nineteenth century 1s—1s 6d was the going rate for the job on the longer tunnels, if job it can be called. Imagine spending a lifetime like 'Ben the

Fig 9 Ben the Legger in 1884

legger' who in fifty years had 'walked' 50—60,000 miles—twice round the world—through Braunston tunnel. It did *him* no harm —he was still sturdy at eighty-six—but many a 'legger' was not so lucky. The 'wings' were about 12in wide by 3ft long and when clipped on to the boat represented something of a perilous position. Many boatmen and 'leggers' met a horrible hidden end.

There was a 'melancholy and distressing catastrophe' on the 'Paddington Canal' (Regent's) in 1825. A Gloucestershire fly-boat entered the Islington tunnel, 'legged' and steered by three men— Russell, George and Williams. Captain Watson walked to the other end with the horses where he waited—with increasing anxiety. Eventually the vessel came out—with no one on board.

> An alarm was given and torches being procured, several boats were manned and entered the tunnel, and about midway Russell was found nearly dead, clinging to a plank, but his comrades had sunk to rise no more. The drags were put in requisition and the body of George was found in a dreadful state having evidently been crushed; but Williams was not found. . . . Russell accounts for the accident by saying they were all working the barge through with their feet . . . lying on a plank, . . . when by some means the plank tilted and they fell into the water, George and Williams uttered a loud cry and he saw them no more; he grasped the plank and saved his life. It was the opinion of some of the navigators, that the men had partaken too freely of the Burton ale on board, and in a drunken state fell overboard. . . .[4]

Drink hastened the end of many a professional legger too. George Bate remembered the leggers who took boats through the tunnels at Tardebigge, Shortwood and King's Norton in the early years of this century.

'These men', he wrote, 'would abide in the Plymouth Arms, a public house situated close to the western end of Tardebigge Tunnel and partake of too much alcoholic liquor to make them unsafe to carry out the job of legging boats.'

Many were drowned.[5]

Legging was unpleasant and dangerous but canal boating in general was only a little less perilous. Death and injury came to the boat people in a host of unexpected, even silly, ways. There was a boatman killed at Smethwick when a drawbridge fell onto his boat because someone had stolen the balance weights.[6] In 1928 a youth stepped up out of a fore cabin and just as his head appeared above the deck the towline of a tug caught him under the chin and flung him into the bottom of the boat. His injuries were such that there was doubt as to whether he would be able to walk again. Two men in separate incidents in 1794 were killed when strong eddies of the tide broke the ropes holding the tillers of their keels and dealt them chance blows. One left a wife and six children. George Hickingbotham, master of the *York Merchant*, met his end in 1826 when the vessel unexpectedly grounded and the sudden shock drove the tiller against his body. Mrs Jones of the *Bee* was critically injured at Trench lock when a windlass left on the pinion by the steerer, flew off and struck her on the head.[7]

Boat people, who usually could not swim, were forever 'taking a look'. One boat woman confessed in 1920 that she had been six times rescued from drowning by her husband. Many did not have such a handy spouse and perished, from drowning or something else. In a short period of time in 1921 a woman lost her life through falling into a lock and being crushed; another was seriously injured through the horse running away, the hauling line breaking and wrapping itself around her legs to drag her from one lock to another; and a captain's wife was badly scalded by boiling water from a kettle upset by the bumping of the boat.[8]

Death stole into some craft in the unwatched hours of the night.

John Hill was master of a very old and very leaky open canal boat which was at her moorings in the river Aire, nearly abreast of Brotherton. He went on board his vessel about nine o'clock at night, with his wife and child; he pumped the water out of the vessel, and they all went to bed. He was heard pumping again about half-past five o'clock; the vessel was discovered sunk in nine feet of water and the three poor inmates perished in the cabin.[9]

Loading and unloading brought their crop of tragedies— Richard Tootle's man killed by a falling rack at Hull as Tootle's sloop was loaded for Sheffield in 1802; Julia Lyth, nineteen, daughter of the steerer of a Shropshire Union boat killed by a faulty crane at Queen's Head Wharf in 1901.[10]

There were collisions too. The hurrying fly-boats often treated other craft with a careless contempt—too careless sometimes. In

1833 one of Messrs Simpson's fly-boats and a coal boat of Mr Pyatt were coming down the canal near Nottingham 'when the rope of the latter got entangled with the fly-boat and completely upset it. The captain, his wife and four children, were all in the cabin at the moment, and it was with considerable difficulty they were rescued from a watery grave'.[11]

Breaches in the canal bank could bring unexpected danger. 'Barnett's Breach' took place at half-past three in the morning on 9 September 1899 when a 100yd of towpath slid into a marl pit 300ft deep belonging to the Stour Valley Brick Works of Mr Samuel Barnett. The waters of the canal poured through the hole carrying down two loaded boats. Fortunately no one was on board. Another boat began to race for the gap and it was only by jumping out and cutting the towrope that the boatman was able to save himself and the horse. Near Dudley Port Station another boat began to be sucked along by the strengthening current. It overtook the horse, which had to follow at an increasing canter. Again the boatman scrambled ashore and, securing a rope round a telegraph pole, saved them all.[12]

The elements brought their own hazards to canals as well as to estuarial waters—wind, flood, fog and ice, especially ice which could nip through the hull of a wooden boat in the course of a night in a strong frost. Boatmen had to carefully break the ice around their boat before retiring. Movement for wooden-hulled craft was dangerous as the jagged ice, even when quite thin, would cut into it. Two barges sunk at Brimscombe forcing a passage through the ice in 1802 were early casualties.[13]

The canal staff were exposed to dangers too, not least in the use of the 'ice-boat'. It was a short iron-hulled craft with a chain running from stem to stern. From the late nineteenth century steel replaced iron and a pole the chain. Men would stand on each side of the chain and rock and heel the boat over to an angle of about 30 degrees. This cracked the ice creating a passage for the boats to follow. Depending upon the thickness of the ice perhaps twenty men would act as 'rockers', the boat pulled by as many as twenty horses steaming with sweat. The boat could rise onto the ice and skitter along on its sides pitching men out on to the frozen canal, or it might fall back at an awkward angle and sink throwing the men into the icy water, which is exactly what happened to the ice boat at work on the Warwick & Birmingham Canal in 1940. Most of the rockers managed to scramble on to the thick ice, but Jess Woodhouse, heavily burdened with winter clothing, disappeared. Fortunately the driver of the last horse unhitched his line, was able to pass it around Jess and drag him out with the horse.[14] In 1854 'as the ice-boat was at work between Fleckmore and Shuckburgh [on the Oxford Canal] the chain broke which the men hold on by, and upwards of twenty of them fell into the canal in which two or three narrowly escaped drowning'.[15]

Lock-keepers were involved in ice-breaking. Mrs Beatrice Birch recalled the days when her husband was a lock-keeper on the Birmingham canals. 'I've seen him with 10 horses each side of the canal rocking the ice-boat to break the ice. They did it to blasts on his whistle.'[16] Joe Green was the *siffleur* in 1940. In that operation a short blast meant haul and the next one stop. Ike Argent recalls how, 'The horses were well trained and acted smartly. Joe was talking with the whistle in his mouth and accidently blew it. He was rolled between the ropes and bridge arch like a rolling pin'.

Lock-keepers were also at risk of falling in as they operated the locks, and some did, although greater familiarity with the idiosyncracies of their own lock reduced the risk as compared with boatmen. There were other hazards for lock-keepers and toll-collectors, as when steerer Cooper 'used Mr Gooden ill' on the Birmingham Canal. Mr Bull, lock-keeper at Smethwick, wrote to complain of the 'ill treatment of John White a steerer of a lime boat'. In another incident the boat *Britania* had not only 'left open a valve' (paddle) but it also had back loading aboard and upon Mr Tildesley 'endeavouring to see what Back Carriage the boat was laden with he was beat and abused'.[17] In 1812 three toll-keepers on the Trent Navigation had to 'be provided with a Blunderbuss and Bayonet at the expense of the Company'. Such incidents can be exaggerated. As boatmen and 'watchmen' came better to understand each others' functions, relations were generally friendly (too friendly for the companies sometimes) characterised by mutual respect, with the odd ill-tempered flare-up between a hurrying boatman and an over zealous lock-keeper or toll-collector. The information that John Prosser, lock-keeper

Plates 23 *and* 24 Hazards: (*above*) an ice-breaker is rocked along an unknown canal. 'Rockers' often got a ducking in the icy water, sometimes with tragic results (*Waterways Museum*); (*below*) boaters sometimes perished when their boat sprang a leak and sank during the night. It was probably a collision which caused this narrow boat of Sephtons' to founder on the Grand Junction in 1911 (*Waterways Museum*)

at Bordesley on the Warwick & Birmingham Canal, who died in 1896, was 'well known and greatly respected by the boatmen of the district', was an epitaph that could have been applied to many others.[18]

In loading and unloading land staff were as much at risk as the boatmen.

> Distressing accident—Last week, as Mr E. Hobson, agent of the River Don Company, at Swinton, assisted by several other persons, was in the act of landing a crate of pots from a vessel lying in the River Dun Cut . . . the roller of the crate fell into the river, and the wheel of the crane struck Mr Hobson violently on the side of his head, knocking him down and fracturing his skull. He remained in a state of insensibility till Friday, when he died.[19]

Lengthsmen, labourers and other maintenance men might be injured or killed in a canal breach or by the giving way of some structure during repairs. Peter Cawley lost his life in a singular way in 1865. Four new ventilation shafts were being built in the Preston Brook tunnel. George Wainwright and Cawley were ordered into the tunnel to do some work on the shafts. They coupled the ice boat to the train of boats being towed through without telling the tug driver expecting to have the job finished by the time the tug returned. They untied the ice boat and began work, but almost immediately they were overcome by the fumes. George Wainwright luckily fell back into the boat, but his companion fell into the water and was drowned.[20]

There were less obvious dangers. Some Birmingham Canal Company workers were sent to investigate rumours of 'depredations' taking place near Junction Bridge in the early hours of an April morning in 1803. They found that the water had been let off and men were endeavouring to take the fish with a net. 'A violent scuffle ensued, and Richard Brothers, one of the Company's servants, was so terribly wounded that he died in the afternoon. Several others were severely bruised.'[21]

In the days before an efficient police force, men were expected physically to defend their master's property and interests, as when a dispute arose between William Pridmore, a farmer, and the Oxford Canal Company. The 'Battle of the Drain' took place in 1817. 'Pridmore brought with him eight men to the drain near the Bridge and had thrown Tiles and Earth all into it together, he stood upon the side of it and pelted the Co's Men as they were in it below him with Sods etc with which he struck six of them out of seven Shuttlewoods Back he has hurt badly.'[22]

Even clerks met their end in company service. All was normal as Henry Barley, a porter with Pickfords, loaded a boat for Wolverhampton at their extensive City Road depot in February 1824. Evening was advancing and in the dimly-lit corner of the warehouse he had difficulty in sorting out two carboys destined for Wednesbury. One broke and its contents ran about the floor. From such a simple accident resulted one of the mightiest conflagrations London had seen for some time. Barley later explained that, 'whilst I was looking at the liquid, one of the men, belonging to the boat, brought a piece of lighted paper over the carboy; I instantly snatched it out of his hand, and it communicated fire to the gas . . . which arose from the liquid . . . and the whole of the carboys were on fire in a minute'.

Three people were trapped in the offices adjoining the warehouse. One of them a clerk called Delcour shouted to the others to make a break for it and himself dived through the flames to safety though he was 'very much burned'. John Veal, a thirty year old collector, 'was so terrified by the fire, that he could not move further and retreated into the office again'. The whole of the warehouse and the offices were soon a mass of flames which were not brought under control until eleven o' clock that night. In the morning Veal's charred unrecognisable body was found. Nearby were the remains of Thomas Evans a fifteen year old clerk.[23]

Thus land workers did suffer accidents from which some of them died, but they were rather exceptional. Their occupation was much less dangerous than that of canal boating.

The cabin of a narrow boat was 'a nice place' too.

'You see many wus places than this in Lunnon,' Captain Jonah remarked proudly.

The exterior was usually aflame with colourful paintings and designs—much more so than on the keels, flats and barges. They were laced with diamond shapes, illustrated with roses and castles and boats sailing upon lakes sheltered beneath mountain ranges. Gaily painted 'dippers' and water cans sat upon the flat roofs, along with wild birds and multi-coloured parrots in cages. Decoration was common to all canal craft. In America

> The pride of the captain and crew in their boats was often enhanced by the gorgeous colouring of the boats exterior. . . . A basin full . . . of boats . . . inevitably exhibited not only the seven colours of the spectrum but symphonies in crimson, maroon, brown, pink, lilac, magenta, yellowish-green, and any other mongrel shade that an experienced mixer of paints might chance to hit upon.[24]

Many interesting theories have been advanced as to the origins of these decorations. One Trent bargeman, whose boat displayed a colour scheme of three contrasting shades, advanced a credible hypothesis. Such combinations were, he reckoned, the result of years of thought, experience and study of boats in their settings and backgrounds.

'One of our greatest problems in navigating the boats', he explained, 'is visibility and spotting the other fellow. The khaki coloured Humber water, gravel banks, grass flood banks, red marl cliffs and dusty mills, all at variance with winter and seasonal

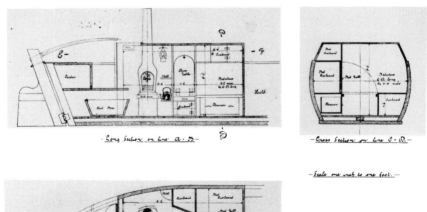

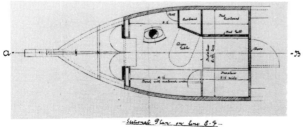

Fig 10 Plan of a narrow-boat cabin (*Director*, NSPCC)

lights, have to be considered in operating a tidal and canal barge.'[25]

But why the traditional decorations? Tony Lewery suggests that they were a spin-off from the cheap everyday art which the advance of industrialisation was putting on to such articles as clocks, trays and furniture. Boat people brightened up their vessels with the current art forms as they came to live more and more on board.

The inside of the narrow-boat cabin was 'small but comfortable, a cosy place to live and sleep in', measuring about 7ft in length, 6ft in width and 6ft in depth. Access was gained from the small flat deck at the 'starn' of the boat through the two gaily painted folding doors surmounted by a lid which slid over the square ventilation hole in the cabin roof—the 'hatches'. A descent of three steps led into the 'room'. On the left was a black chubby stove, usually brightly polished and in full glow. Nearly above the stove was a small oil or paraffin lamp. Next to the stove was a cupboard of several shelves, where the crockery was kept. A brightly painted door, studded with shining brass knobs, was hinged to shut up the shelves or let down horizontally to form a table. On the right of the cabin, opposite the stove and cupboard was a seat about 4ft long and 18in wide. This served as the 'side bed' for children and for the 'chap'. At the end of the cabin was the 'bedroom'—a wooden seat, about 3ft wide extending across the width of the cabin. This space could be shut off by neatly-drawn curtains or wooden sliding doors. In the unoccupied space there were more brass knobs and hooks for hanging up clothes, ropes, a whip and other sundry articles. The kitchen and cooking utensils hung gracefully on hooks behind the stove. The place was 'gay with paint. There were vignettes of Rhine castles on the neat lockers, and roses everywhere'. Every inch of space was crammed with odd articles—a pair of tiny brass candlesticks, an American clock, half a dozen small coloured prints, a choice selection of 'In Memoriam' cards framed and glazed, often replaced in more recent times by photographs. Lace work was another more recent addition. Wherever a piece of metal was visible it invariably shone.

This very often was the only home of the boatman and his family. Here were enacted the romances, the comedies and the tragedies of their lives. 'You might visit a worse place than a boat

Plates 25 and 26 Interiors: (above) keelman and his son in their cabin. Keel cabins were not usually decorated as lavishly as the narrow-boat cabins (Leeds Library); (below) a narrow-boat stove and its surroundings (John Stevenson)

cabin,' Mr Clarke concluded in 1922 and one boat builder in 1877 reckoned there were 'places in London that are fifty thousand times worse in regard to space and cleanliness than the boat cabins are. Look down Limehouse and about there . . .'.[26]

But when the Medical Officer of the Port of Manchester made observations on boat cabins in 1925 it was not their colour which impressed him, nor did he compare them favourably with the slums of Limehouse. Instead he laid emphasis upon the weakness of the chests of the people who lived in them. He acknowledged the liability of the boatman to fatal accident, but this alone did not account for his 'extraordinarily' high position—above farm labourers and fishermen—in the mortality tables. 'What really appears to carry him off . . . is his liability to pneumonia and other respiratory diseases,' Dr Dearden concluded.[27]

Many boats had no ventilation except the hatchway and the stove pipe. Some had a diamond shaped 'day-light hole' about $2\frac{1}{2}$in each way through to the cargo space, but this was often blocked up by the cargo or by the boat people themselves for 'it was the custom to close the "bit" up at night and literally exclude the air!' The hatchway was also closed at night and during damp weather, making the cabin stuffy, a situation exacerbated by the fierce little stove. 'With reasonable air inlets,' Dr Dearden explained, 'this stove will function successfully as the main outlet for ventilation, but when, under certain circumstances, there are no inlets acting, the stove provides a considerable risk of carbon monoxide poisoning.'

The *Standard* reporter put it differently. He stepped into a narrow-boat cabin 'but only to step out again . . . the atmosphere of the place was simply stifling. And here during the best part of the night had slept the boatman, his wife, two children, and the wife's male relative . . .'.

A reporter of the *Birmingham Daily Mail* in March 1875 was 'puzzled to know how the boat people can stand such sudden changes of temperature. They come out of an overheated cabin on to the exposed cabin top; when the family retire for the night the cabin is usually suffocatingly hot, and as the fire goes out, in cold weather, it cools to a very low temperature . . . I should fear that lung diseases are common . . .'.

He heard 'of some terrible tales of sickness and death, gaunt tragedies hidden from the unthinking world in those little flat-topped cabins that we pass without a second thought'. Boat life was 'bitter bad in sickness', one boat woman lamented.

'When there are infectious cases among the boat people there is not the slightest chance of isolation; every person in the cabin is continually coming in contact', the NSPCC report for 1925–6 pointed out.

There was, for instance, the captain of the boat *Tangmere* very ill with consumption in 1926. For two years the NSPCC officer tried to persuade him to go to a sanatorium, but he always refused. His wife, two children and a lad of twelve lived in the same cabin. It was frequently pointed out to him how bad this was for the other occupants, but to no avail. Eventually, when the boat was at Ellesmere Port, the man became so ill that he was unable to get up and was removed to hospital where he died. Fortunately the others escaped unscathed.

Among all the boat people there was this reluctance to have to do with doctors and they had an even greater fear of hospitals, partly because of their insularity, but also because they involved delay. As one boatman said, 'he would lose a day's wage every day he lay there'. 'We just stay sick until we get well,' an American boatman explained.

The *Corinthian* was tied up in the Hay Basin at Wolverhampton, again in 1926. In the cabin were the captain's wife and two very small children, all seriously ill. A doctor reckoned that the only chance the woman and children had of recovering was immediate removal to hospital. The captain did not want his wife to go to hospital. Nor did she want to go.

'I have done my best,' the doctor told the NSPCC Inspector, 'as also have the Sanitary Inspector and Relieving Officer, to persuade them to go, but they still refuse.'

The NSPCC man managed to persuade them to go. All recovered and returned to the boat, except the elder girl aged ten, who stayed with her grandmother and went to school. Not all such incidents ended so happily.

There were other aspects of the life which might be fruitful ground for disease. Cubbon asked young Harry Theobalds if there were any rats on his boat.

'Yes, dozens!' he replied, 'which we keep out of the cabins by closing the sliding doors. At night they run about the roof: but they do you no harm!'

Some cargoes were not very conducive to good health. One vessel met with in Sheffield was loaded with old hoofs, horns etc 'the stench from which was unbearable . . .'. The boards of the flooring of the cabin of another boat, carrying London slop in 1887, was found to be completely saturated. There was 3in of fluid under the floor, and the 'smell in the cabin was exceedingly offensive'. Manure was a common cargo, and it was almost inevitable that the cabins of such vessels should become verminous. Intermittent 'bug driving'—closing all the apertures and burning brimstone in the cabin—was for long the only, and not very satisfactory, method of reducing the unpleasant inmates until legislation in 1877 and 1884 enforced a double bulkhead in such boats and empowered sanitary inspectors to fumigate them more scientifically. This reduced the problem. It did not completely eradicate it, for 'de-bugging' continued to be necessary right up to the end of carrying.

Pure water for drinking, cooking and washing was another problem. One medical officer of health enquiring as to where the boat people got their water was told 'from the canal. In this district, at least, this water is unfit for drinking or cooking purposes, but beyond the boundary of it the master of this boat said the quality was better'.

'It is to be regretted', wrote John Brydone, 'that there are not available pumps along the different waterways . . . for the supply of this absolute necessity of life of a pure quality. . . .' There would be another advantage he added as 'the provision of good water might keep many a boatman from the public house'.[28]

Washing of clothes and people—for 'those that do wash', George Smith wrote scathingly—was difficult, given the problems of water supply and the confined quarters in which they lived. And boat people were generally thought to be 'deficient in sanitary knowledge'. Again it was a problem of their living conditions, for there were no toilets on the boats and very few available by the canal side. The canal or the 'other side of the hedge', was the boat people's toilet, but there was not always a hedge, especially in large towns.

Nor was it on every boat that the boat and cabin were neatly painted; every piece of metal burnished; the cabin a model of cleanliness and order. Some sank beneath the difficulties of the life. Certain areas had more slum boats than others. Many of those in the neighbourhood of Runcorn in 1877 were, according to the *Standard* reporter, 'filthy to a degree, and in many cases utterly unfit for human habitation'. The very worst he ever saw were the 'flats' bringing coal from Wigan along the Bridgewater Canal— 'the Wigan "flats" are out and out the very worst, and the Wigan boat people the most depraved'. Many Runcorn boats were still considered particularly bad in the 1920s as were some trading in and near the Metropolis. Indeed slum boats survived until the demise of canal carrying in the 1960s.

'Their cabins', remarked Sister Hanson in 1961, 'are either spotless or the reverse.'[29]

'The romance of canal life has been overdone,' one reporter concluded in 1923. 'When you look into it there is not much left but hard work, monotony, and privation. The pictures on the cabin tops and the gaudy buckets are the gilt on a hard gingerbread.'[30]

8
The Larnin' Question

The hardships and dangers of waterway life fell nowhere more heavily and tragically than upon the innocent minds and bodies of those who could least bear them. It is a salutary thought that much of the economy of canal transport, certainly in this century, rested on the limbs of children of tender years. The same could be said of foreign waterways. 'If it weren't for the children the canal wouldn't run a day,' one American boatman admitted in 1922. It was a vexed question to many observers.[1]

The dangers were magnified. For many children the picturesque cabins were death traps and 'hell holes'. 'The wonder is', wrote the *Standard* reporter after listening to Captain Jonah's proud description of the sleeping arrangements in his cabin, 'that the children have not long since been stifled in their cupboard beds, or smothered by the overlying of the parents.'

What is even more amazing is that such cabins often contained not the two children and 'chap' as in Captain Jonah's boat, but sometimes six, seven and even nine in addition to the parents. There were fatalities resulting from people sleeping huddled together in such a confined ill-ventilated space. Babies like young Joseph Huskisson were particularly at risk. He was found dead in the cabin of a boat at Runcorn in 1877. It turned out that the mother and three children had been sleeping in a bed barely the size of an ordinary table.[2]

The width of the bed in the *Tasmania* was 34in, the sleeping place of a father, mother and one month-old child in 1921, resulting in the death of young William Roberts through suffocation.[3] A similar case occurring in 1920 demonstrated some of the sad inconveniences of canal-boat life, for when a police officer went to inspect the body of a dead baby the boatman's wife, who

Fig 11 Interior of a narrow-boat cabin, 1884

was lying ill in bed, produced it from under her pillow. She did not know where else to put the little body so as to remove it from the sight of her other children.

A cramped moving home, containing two potential hazards like a stove and an oil lamp, prey to fierce unexpected draughts, surrounded by so many combustible items, was not the safest of dwellings. Within easy reach of small hands they accounted for many on the long list of children whose needless deaths featured fleetingly, but endlessly through the newspapers, like the eighteen month old boy who pulled over the paraffin lamp when he was alone (his parents were on deck) in the cabin of a keel tied up at Rotherham Wharf in 1910. His clothes caught fire and he died.

'Hetty is on fire,' screamed a terrified child from below decks on another keel as it approached Thorne in the same year. Hetty's mother rushed below to find her daughter a mass of flames. Quickly she rolled her in a rug, but it was too late—she died the next day. At the inquest it was assumed that the wind must have blown the flames out of the fire, the child's clothes being set alight. The coroner was forthright in his criticism of the unfortunate parents. The floor was a wooden one and there was no protection of any description from the fire. It was a shocking thing that the parents should be so neglectful. The father replied sadly, and truthfully, that there was very little space.[4]

In the even more confined narrow-boat cabins accidents from

126

burning were still more frequent. One two year old child in 1927 was playing with a celluloid toy on the side bed as his mother was putting dinner into the oven. The toy got near the fire and burst into flames. The child immediately threw the toy away, but it fell on the face of the baby, which was so badly burned that it died. The space between the stove and the side bed was about two feet! This also explains why it was so easy for a five year old boy to scald himself fatally in the following year. He accidentally knocked a boiling kettle off the stove with his clothing as he got dressed.

Scalding was a frequent cause of injury and death not only because the boat was a work place but a moving one. Bumps and bangs often caused upsets from the stove. One captains wife nursed a baby in the cabin of a boat being loaded at Ellesmere Port in 1925. A heavy package fell from the crane on to the side of the boat, causing a sudden list. A boiling kettle fell off the stove; water cascaded over the baby and it died. One family lost three children through scalding.

Children were forever falling into the canal too. In 1927 of 34 children questioned at the special school at Brentford 23 admitted to having fallen into the 'cut' at one time or another.[5] One boy of eleven was known to have been in the canal 18 times. He was lucky, for many were 'drownded'. One boy of nine fell from his boat at Brentford in the night. Falling head first he stuck in the mud and was suffocated before he could be found.

Like their parents, few of the children could swim. The story is told of a schools' inspector who visited the special school for canal-boat children at Norwood Green, near Bulls Bridge in the 1950s.

'These children need exercise,' he told the school teacher sternly. 'Why don't they bring their tennis rackets?'

Their teacher explained spiritedly thar if there was one thing they were not short of it was exercise and how much better it would be for them if they learned to swim. It was in fact agreed that swimming lessons should be laid on and the parents were written to for permission to go to the baths. Several replied in the same vein.

'Us don't want our kids to go to them barfs; us'll barf 'em us selfs.'

Five or six children did learn to swim, however.

The list of accidents is endless and this is before the deaths and injuries caused by children working the boats are taken into account, for there is no doubt that the children did work and worked very hard. Harry Fletcher has written of some of the hardships and dangers that he endured as a keel boy in the early years of this century. In the 1920s very young children—as young as six—could still be seen steering the boat, standing on a stool so that they could reach the tiller. Sometimes they got knocked off. One girl of twelve had her arm crushed between the tiller and the hatchways suffering a fracture which put her in hospital for six weeks. Horses were a frequent cause of injury and death. A lad of seven suffered a badly fractured skull when the horse he was driving, startled by some bathers, turned round and bolted the way it had come, gathering up the boy in the loop of the towline and dashing his head against the side of the boat.

Lock work, loading and unloading brought still more accidents —to children like Ernest Morris, a ten year old who had his fingers damaged by the cogs of a crane wheel whilst the *Quail* was being unloaded in 1900.[6]

A study of children on an American canal revealed much the same situation.[7]

It was not that canal-boat parents were cruel by nature—'They seldom actively ill-treat them . . .', commented the *Child's Guardian* in June 1910—although some did. It was rather unthinking ignorance and sometimes necessity which led them to encourage their children to labour along with them as they had done with their fathers.

One keel captain advised the NSPCC officer in 1929,

You want to go up to Doncaster Dyke, Mister, there'll you see boats with 5 or 6 kids. I have met them there fastened to the boat by the hauling line, hauling a boat full of coal for miles. Their parents neither have horse nor mate. It is a disgrace for everybody for it to be allowed.

Another captain told the officer,

The Board of Trade ought to stop the little children from working on canal boats, I leave my children at home. It is a wretched shame that children should be made to work like they do; there ought to be more Inspectors looking after the kids. I hope they get them off the boats. Those who say it is such a healthy life ought to see the things we see—kids working late at night, sometimes all night, in cold, wet and foggy weather.

The health of boat children (and boat people) had always been something of a controversial question. No children were more healthy or more sick according to which observer was consulted.

According to the NSPCC, boat people were careless of their children's

> . . . health and cleanliness and they are slow to provide medical attention when it is required . . . thorough and frequent cleansing of the skin is essential to the well-being of a child, but on a canal boat the facilities for bathing and washing the children are of the poorest description, and the result is that a wash is not a daily occurrence. . . . The result of all this is that the children are pallid (when their colour is visible), dull-eyed and listless.

In the 1950s and 1960s one nurse found the canal folk hard to teach.

'They stuff a bottle in a baby's mouth when it cries, bath it sometimes and never weigh it.'

'The surprising result,' she did add, 'is that it usually grows up into a fine, sturdy youngster.'[8]

Others, however, had an answer as to why so many of the older children and adults often seemed to be so hardy. 'Like the Spartans, most of the boatmen and boatwomen are people of iron constitution, and probably for the same reason . . .'—ie weaklings were eliminated by the rigours of the life.

Certainly many did perish for one reason or another. One coroner enquiring into the death of a boatman's child found that it was the last of a family of fourteen all dead. Of another family, eight children had died and in another six children were alive out of a family of fifteen.[9] One American mother had lost four children on canal boats. The oldest child had died of 'sunstroke'; the second, five years of age, had been drowned; another had been burned to death by an explosion of oil on the barge; another, a baby, had died of spinal meningitis after being dropped on the deck of the boat. One of the surviving children had been injured by the oil explosion which killed the third child.[10]

It was not always completely the interests of the children that brought complaint for their being on board—although such complaints were probably sincere enough. There was an element of self-interest too.

'It is stopping other boatmen from getting jobs,' complained one boatman in 1929 'and it hadn't ought to be allowed; too little children are set to work, they ought to be at school.'

People who made a genuine sacrifice to keep their children at home resented the unfair competition from those who did not.

'I leave my wife and children at home and pay three men to help me work my two boats,' explained one narrow-boat captain. 'If I can do this and make a living, so ought the others.'

There was general agreement among men in a similar position. It is not surprising that the Transport and General Workers Union opposed the practice of women and children living-in on canal boats.

If children found life hard with their parents, it must have been still harder for those who worked with others. 'It's a very common thing for them to be lending their children from one boat to another,' a canal missionary told the *Standard* reporter, 'boys and girls both . . .', an opinion expressed by others down into the 1930s. This was often to relatives where the children were treated little worse than if they had been with their parents, but there were some poor children, who, in order to ease the overcrowding in a cabin or help the family budget, were given away, even sold, to other boat people regardless of the consequences. This was often strenuously denied, and the practice was largely restricted to the north-west Midlands, but it did occur; a girl of ten lent to the captain of a boat to drive the horse at Wolverhampton in 1924; a boy of eleven lent to another captain at Stoke-on-Trent, and so on.

The canals had always been something of a catching ground for waifs and strays. Some were bad boys—in 1841, 'such boys who have run away from their parents or committed some improper Act . . . frequently these Boys have robbed their masters and then run away from them'.[11] There were said to be 'some awfully precocious specimens of depravity' among the boys on the

American canals according to the missionaries there, though such men sometimes had a rather distorted view of 'depravity'.[12] Some boys were kidnapped and treated almost as slaves by boatmen who could not find labour to work their boat. In 1839 Edward King, when he was about eight years old, was 'stolen' by a Manchester fly-boat captain at the Fishery Lock, Boxmoor. For three years he worked on the canals far from his home, but eventually the boat again headed for London and he was promised that he would be allowed to see his parents at Boxmoor. The boatman broke his promise, took away the boy's trousers and shut him in the cabin. Edward found a way out and ran home without his trousers.[13]

Some were poor boys and orphans . . . like George Blakemore who was tragically drowned in 1910 in the Trent & Mersey Canal. He was, however, not quite the boy he appeared to be.

> Placed in the coffin, the body was left awaiting possible identification. Prompted by curiosity, a lad, also working on a canal boat went to view the body, when he found it was not George Blakemore but his brother, who would be thirteen years old in November. The lad who thus identified his brother had himself been absent from home for four months, and had not been seen during that time by his parents.[14]

One boy who came on to the canals under special circumstances really was an orphan. A Norwegian schooner was wrecked off the Cornish coast in the late nineteenth century. The survivors were brought to Bristol and among them was a flaxen-haired infant whose parents had been drowned. A childless couple on a boat offered to take him. As the ship had been wrecked near Padstow and as he came from Norway it was as Paddy North that he was launched upon the canals.[15]

There is little doubt that the lives of such children (excluding Paddy North as it happens) could be a misery. The boy (and sometimes the girl) became the scapegoat for the captain's frustrations (sometimes it was the horse)—not only during the Canal Age but, since the canals were often hidden from the public gaze and inspectors were late in coming to the canal banks, down into quite recent times too. A boatman who sold his son to another boatman wrote a letter to him in 1903.

Tell — Northwich cruelty man is after you about Fred [aged 10] not going to school and being illtreated he has been to me to-day a bout it and runcorn cruelty man was with him.

The Northwich cruelty man say you have him for as slave you had better let me have him as soon as you can and I will go with you to them to stop them from going to law. The are wactting you night and day the tould me not write to you the wants cath you the have been waching the boats the told me has you have him up at half past tow in the morning. . . .[16]

Even as late as the 1920s and 1930s their misery continued. A keel captain 'saw that Captain H.C. with those two little boys he had given to him; they are no relation to him, he works them like slaves. I saw him knock one of the boys about last week. . . . He works the children from early morning to dark—hail, rain and snow'.

One bargeman, however, on the Leeds & Liverpool Canal, got back more than he bargained for when he savagely attacked his fourteen year old assistant at Leigh. This captain forced the boy to strip and then he kicked him, burst his nose and bruised him with his fists. 'Hearing the boy's screams a collier went to his assistance. The lad was bleeding from the nose and ears and both eyes were discoloured. The collier recovered the lad's clothing and then finished up by "pummelling" the captain,' who was also later fined £10 and £4 costs.[17]

The most regrettable part of the canal–boat child's life was that his access to education was so limited. 'There's many thousands of 'em on the canals that doesn't know a letter in the book', one concerned boat mother remarked in 1877. She would be glad enough to have her children educated if she could and get away from the boat life. She was tired of it.[18]

George Smith made an issue of the education of the boat children and was successful in getting education clauses inserted into the Canal Boats Acts of 1877 and 1884. Mr Parr considered the results of the Acts A DEAD FAILURE by 1910. Children were supposed to go to school where the boat had been registered. Since many boats never revisited their place of registration parents would obtain a certificate authorizing the attendance of the children at some other more convenient place. 'I have known parents to have more than one [certificate],' Parr complained,

> . . . and assure the School Attendance Officer in Sandbach that the children were attending school at Runcorn, and then equally success-fully convince the officer at Runcorn that the children were being taught at Sandbach . . .; they are some of the worst educated people in the kingdom, after thirty-six years of compulsory education.

To prevent such evasions the boat people were often issued with a book wherein school attendances were marked, and if there were insufficient a fine was imposed. Where there *was* school attendance it was rarely continuous. One day the children might attend school, the next few days they might be on the boat, and then spend another half day in a school 50 miles away. 'I can't go to school because the boat always goes on', one boat boy complained.

Little wonder that by 1899, after twenty-two years of trying to cope with the problem, even those education authorities which had made keen efforts to solve it were 'subsiding into the inaction of despair'.

The net result was that many in the generation of boaters that grew up in the years after the passing of the Acts were as illiterate as their fathers. The NSPCC reported disparagingly on evidence of illiteracy in the 1920s. One father described his son as being 'a grand scholar', but he failed to spell 'news'. Another boy, described as a 'good sharp scholar', when asked if he knew the alphabet, inquired what it was.

Wherever there were canal and river boats involved in long journeys there was this problem of schooling. In America, even though many of the canals were closed for several months during the winter more than 'three fourths of the children 8 years of age or over who had attended school during the year 1920–21 were one or more years retarded; over one-half were two years or more below the normal grade for their age', because of the irregularity of attendance.[19] In France too in the 1920s it was realised that the majority of waterway children were illiterate. The Dutch were in the van with the education of their floating population from the early years of this century. There was a movement afoot to adopt the 'Holland Scheme' (including boarding schools) in Britain in the late 1920s, but nothing came of it, probably for the same reason that earlier less ambitious suggestions had collapsed—ie who was to pay the extra costs of educating boat children?[20]

By the 1920s, however, the problem was lessening in Britain in the sense that there were far fewer children 'living-in'. Special schools for boat children had been opened at such places as Paddington and Brentford where the boats tended to lie for longer periods, unloading or waiting a cargo. A few school teachers in ordinary schools did begin to look more favourably upon the passing boat children—at Braunston, in Birmingham, and Ellesmere Port for instance—and the boat people were encouraged to send their children to such schools. A surprising number of children learned the rudiments of reading and writing during a period of prolonged illness, or during an extended stoppage through a strike or frost, or when, in more recent years, boats were tied up for three months during a confinement. The boat people were beginning to appreciate more the disadvantages of being uneducated. Dejected talk was heard among young men who had lost the chance of a good job because they were unable to read or write. 'Master, we would give twenty pounds this minute if we could read and write,' they told Mr Clarke in 1922. In consequence parents strove much harder to see that their children got to school when they could. They often left them with friends or relatives on shore. Local authorities seemed to be more alive to their duty with regard to canal-boat children. Illiterate adults were increasingly anxious to get their children educated—'it is the exception nowadays who are unable to read and write,' Llewellyn concluded in 1923.[21]

Even so, according to J. I. Watts of the NSPCC, over the period 1920–9 only a quarter of the canal-boat children of school age

Plates 27 *and* 28 Canal children—danger, hardship and lack of education were the main drawbacks to their life. Two solutions: (*above*) one of the last of the canal children tied to the cabin roof of a narrow boat moored at Dickinson's paper mill on the (new) Grand Union, 1967 (*Daily Telegraph*); (*below*) Mrs Purvis with canal children at their special school, Norwood Green, 1962 (*Mrs C. Purvis*)

were considered to be 'educated', and as late as 1952 children like twelve year old Gertie Berridge, found working a Clayton gas boat in Birmingham, were by no means exceptional. She had never been to school and could neither read nor write.[22]

There was considerable debate about the meaning of the word 'education'. Llewellyn *was* concerned about the lack of education of the boat children and he often remarked upon it, but at the same time he stressed how the life was an education in itself. 'Undoubtedly those ashore are more fully equipped in the matter of learning, but in the application of it I do not think most of them have any advantage over the boat children.' While children ashore were still at play those on the boats were to be 'found doing their duty in a quiet matter of fact way, and taking a pride in its successful accomplishment'.[23] 'Many of these boat children,' reported the NSPCC's officer, 'although unable to read or write are sharp in many other ways and show keen intelligence.' They were naturally good at mental arithmetic. 'You needn't teach them a thing about money,' said Mrs Purvis.

At their special schools they showed an aptitude for design and a feeling for colour. They all loved painting and embroidery, including the boys. They particularly liked music and dancing. Those who got to know the boat children found their natural and unaffected ways very engaging. They were direct about matters that other children would be reticent about. At a party at the Norwood Green school two blancmanges, a cream rose bud on each, were carried shivering through the room. As one the children burst into uncontrolled laughter. The teacher eventually asked a small boy where the joke was.

'Don't they look like tits?' he piped up unashamedly. They told intimate stories of their home life quite freely. If they did not like something they said so, but there was a readiness to co-operate and an absence of hooliganism that was often lacking in the children of more sophisticated families.

The long years of attempting to get the children educated by the NSPCC, the TGWU and others seemed finally about to bear fruit in 1930. A Labour government was in power and a Private Member's Bill was brought before Parliament. Considering that it was a measure which would affect only about 400 families and perhaps 1,500 children, there was a surprising amount of opposition to it. The debate in the Commons was particularly emotional:

> Colonel Wedgwood: My complaint against this Bill is that it embodies in it a proposal to take the children away from their homes.
> Mr Sexton: Do you call these places homes?
> Colonel Wedgwood: Where the father and mother are living there is the home.
> Mr Sexton: You go and live there!
> Colonel Wedgwood: You go and live at St. Helens!
> Mr Speaker: I think we should get on better, and certainly in a more dignified manner, if we conducted the Debate a little quieter.
> Colonel Wedgwood: The real difficulty is that this bill involves taking the children away from their homes.
> Mr Sexton: Homes! Prisons! Convict cells!
> Colonel Wedgewood: My point is that under the Education Acts—
> Mr Sexton: I am ashamed of you. I am going out of the house.
> Colonel Wedgwood: That is an exposition of—
> Mr Palin: We are all ashamed of you—absolutely ashamed of you. [Both were Labour MPs]
> Mr Speaker: Will hon. Members allow the right hon. Gentleman to proceed.[24]

No less a distinguished institution than *The Times* descended, on 9 May, from mightier concerns to add its weight to the campaign. 'In the sacred name of education . . .,' it pronounced,

> . . . the House of Commons is asked to break up the homes and destroy the family life of a class of kindly, law-abiding citizens, with standard of decency and morality not always to be found in the crowded slums to which, if the Bill goes through, many of these children, in the most impressionable years of their lives, will probably be banished.

In an age when, after several decades of compulsory education, some people feared that the nation was becoming regimented to the dictates of the State—'chiselled into the artificial and unnatural conditions of town life'—they rather enjoyed the thought that some were able to cheat the system. Perhaps there was a certain envy of the Bohemian freedom of canal-boat life.

The following letter appeared in *The Times* of Thursday, 20 February 1930, under the heading 'Children of the canals' and the sub-heading 'If the Bill becomes law':

To the Editor of *The Times*

Sir,—We are canal-boat people, with children to feed and clothe. Will you give us room in your paper to show what Mr. Gosling's Bill will do to us and them?

Some of the boats are our own, others are rented from the employers or provided by them. Some are towed by horses, others by tugs. Whether we are working for contractors or for ourselves, we are carriers, and have to compete with the railways and with road motors. If canal freights are raised, our loads will go on to the roads or the railways. This keeps our wages down. And though by working long hours we manage to make a living, most of us have little to spare at the end of the week. We can just manage because we work in families, and everyone helps who can.

The Bill says no children under 15 are to be allowed on the barges. This will mean they will have to live on land. Where can they live? We cannot pay for good lodgings: they will have to crowd into cheap ones. If the mother goes with them, someone else will have to help to work the boat. There are some families whose children will be old enough to stay, but there are many who will not. These families will have to keep a home for mother and children on land, and another for father on the boat, and get someone else to help on the boat as well. Two homes on one wage: we cannot do it.

What is to become of these people? Mrs. X, a widow with four children, eldest 10, youngest 2, works the boat herself and keeps her family. Miss R, orphan, with brother 13 and sister 7, works the boat herself and keeps all three. Mr. and Mrs. Y, own two boats: five children under 15, two over: cannot keep two homes on what they earn. Mr. and Mrs. Z, (boat provided), four children under 15, one over 15, on boat; would have to go on the dole.

A great deal is said about the refuse boats. People forget that refuse is large stuff that does not blow about as much as dust. A refuse boat is not as bad for people's health as the dirty, dusty streets near Euston or a Paddington slum. Though we work on refuse boats, we are clean and our children are healthy. We help to keep London's homes clean; we serve others, and we ask them to help us. Times are bad, and will be for some years. A better way would be to leave us where we are and provide more schools for our children. To-day there are only two—at Paddington and Brentford. We could do with one at Yiewsley and several in the Midlands, one at Leeds and at Manchester. The special canal schools are easier for the children. While so many are out of work it does seem mad to turn us out of our homes.

This letter is written at a meeting of canal-boat people. Signed for all of us.

ELIZABETH KING, Excelsior.
SAMUEL CAVE, Kingfisher.
ELLEN FARRER, Industry.
FREDERICK WHEELER, Penguin.
Canal Boatmen's Institute, Paddington.

The following Wednesday, 26 February 1930, this letter appeared, also under the heading 'Children of the canals':

To the Editor of *The Times*

Sir,—Of the men and women working on the canals, there is a very large section whose attitude is in no way represented by the letter published in your columns to-day. In Cheshire, for instance, these workers complain bitterly of the conditions in which they are forced to bear and rear their children on the barges. Many of the families actually have cottages somewhere at the canal side, but can very rarely go to them, because the father of the family needs help to manage his boat, and receives too small a weekly wage to enable him to pay an assistant. The women ask why in this trade alone it should be necessary for them and their children to provide unpaid labour in order that the men may be able to earn a living or, indeed, follow their trade at all.

I venture to suggest that all the arguments raised to keep children on the canals are precisely those used 100 years ago to keep children working in mines and factories. It was said that the family could not live without the children's work: that the children themselves were far better off because they had better food if they worked; that the trade could not be carried on without their work because times were bad. Is there anyone to-day who doubts the wisdom of having removed the children from industry to educate them, or who contends that children are not physically and mentally better and healthier as a result? Yet because one class of children have, as it were, been overlooked, and are still in the dark ages, uneducated and forced to work from babyhood, all the old arguments are revived, with as much—or as little—force as 100 years ago.

Your correspondents give a number of 'hard cases' to prove the necessity of keeping the children on the canals. Let me quote one from my own experience on the other side. Mrs. T—living on a barge with her husband and two children, gave birth to a third child on the barge. The only accommodation for the whole family was a cabin 5ft. 2in. high, a little over 6ft. wide, and about 8ft. long: in this cabin the whole family ate and slept; here the washing, mending, cooking and cleaning were done, and here the baby was born. Are we to believe that this family would be worse and not better off if its members lived in a cottage ashore, with the father coming back when on leave, as happens with every other class of sailor or waterman? The children would then not have to grow up illiterate, but, having education, would be able, if they so wished, to adopt some other trade. At present this is impossible, because nowhere can they compete with the boys and girls who can read and write.

It may be that there are some men and women on the canals who wish the old bad conditions to prevail. I do not know; I have not met them; but even if it is so, it is no argument for the continuance of those conditions.

Yours, &c..

BARBARA AYRTON GOULD.

1, Hamilton-terrace, N.W.8. Feb. 20.

Harry Gosling, himself an ex-waterman and a trade union MP, asked his fellow members to keep out of their minds 'What some silly fools have been writing in the "Times" and other papers about these children'. Another continued 'All these fancy idyllic stories which have been in the Press in the last two or three days backed up with those beautiful photographs of country scenes, may be all very well, but the real facts are not as depicted there'.[25] It was all to no avail since the Bill was defeated.

Several middle class women's organisations actively opposed the Bill on the grounds that the clause forbidding women and children to live on boats carrying foul and dangerous cargoes interfered with the equality of the sexes.[26]

L. T. C. Rolt writing amid the 'innumerable restrictions, regulations and difficulties . . .' of the period of another (the post-war) Labour government—'when education and material amenities are the shibboleths of our ardent social reformers'—captured the spirit of the philosophy of the opposition with his eloquent pen. We were 'struggling to be kings' at the expense of such 'independence, self reliance, fellowship and pride . . .' as the canal boaters possessed, aided by the 'zealous reformer, intent as always on minding everybody's business but his own . . .'.[27]

Tom Cubbon might have echoed such sentiments in the 1920s. He too remarked on the maturity and self reliance of the boat children and upon one in particular. Near Chester he and his wife tied up by a grain boat

> . . . in charge of a boy about fourteen years of age, rejoicing in the name of Harry Theobald, whose face—and style also—were more in accordance with an embryo bishop than a budding bargee. . . . The greatness of the boy's attitude was something to marvel at! His silent way of acting first, and talking afterwards, with a quiet assurance of manner worthy of a Kitchener, must have been handed down to him by a long line of great ancestors; and we often picture him in future days guiding victorious armies in the field, or reading momentous speeches through steel-rimmed spectacles.

But Harry Theobalds became neither general nor bishop. He remained a boatman. Probably he would never have wanted to be either soldier or churchman, but he was never, like many other canal-boat children, given the opportunity. They were condemned to continue in the style of their fathers and when the demise of canal transport meant that they could no longer carry on that vocation many, because of their lack of education, were at a distinct disadvantage.

The much vaunted maturity and self reliance was achieved through necessity and by ordeal. The life was hard and dangerous and under such circumstances the survivors grew up before their time. The boat children had no childhood.

'They didn't know how to play,' Mrs Purvis recalls. 'They couldn't do "ring-a-roses". They were not interested in football or things like that.' There was little time and few facilities for the normal pursuits of children. They were conditioned by the need to work. A working life is long enough without its encroaching into childhood years and the fact that it did so upon the canals until only a few years ago was really untenable . . . and rather disgraceful.

9
The Guv'nor

'Look you,' complained Captain Jonah as he voyaged up the Grand Junction Canal in 1877, 'things could not be wuss with me and mine than they is at present. . . . It's as much as us can do to make both ends meet now.'

It would be a good thing he reckoned if children were banned from the boats.

'If they takes the children they take in course the mothers, and if they takes the mothers that means rising the wages. D'yer see!'

A Runcorn boat woman—an 'Amazon with tanned face and goodly beard'—put the same point rather differently, but more forcefully. She began,

> Master, they's got to recompense us. They's got to gi' us more money. They'll 'ave to do som'at for us when they taks the childr'n out of the boats, or us can never live. The masters w'll have to find the 'orses . . ., and they'll have to pay the boatmen reg'lar weekly wages. That's what they's got to do. We w'd like to be ashore and 'ave the childr'n to school; but us can't live ashore without more wages.

' 'Er's right,' agreed the onlooking boat people. 'Sal knows on 't. Leave 'er alone for knowin' about us.'

The *Standard* reporter came to the conclusion that the 'wages question' was in fact the 'one great hinge on which everything seems to turn', and Runcorn women were saying much the same in 1920.

Criticism fell upon the employers who allowed such poor rewards and bad living and working conditions. The Reverend John Davies' praise of some employers of boatmen in 1841 was by implication a condemnation of others.

Those who feel an Interest in their Men and look upon them in a different Light from the Horses that drag the Boats, remembering that they are immortal Beings—those Masters have discrimination, and can see that the more . . . Priveleges are granted . . . the greater generally their improvement.[1]

George Smith had some harsh words to say about the employers as he strove, not always fairly, to get his Canal Boats Bills onto the Statute Book and then enforced. In 1930 one Labour MP saw morals, decency and education 'being butchered to make a Roman holiday for . . . private enterprise'. Harry Gosling was more specific:

There is a gentleman of importance in the transport world, Mr Fane de Salis, who speaks on behalf of the Canal Association, and he says this:
'We admit the children are not educated, that education is the weak point; they do not get it, we admit it.'
For a man just to say that, and then go home and go to bed, is beyond me. If they do admit it, and they are people of importance and they do represent the Canal Association, I should feel inclined . . . to say to them 'Why the devil do you let it go on if you admit it, if you so frankly admit it, if you say it is beyond any question?'[2]

There was some justification for such criticisms, but they have left a written record of unfeeling employers that perhaps does less than justice to the 'guv'nors'.

Despite much that has been written on the canal companies and on such famous carrying firms as Pickfords, Worthington & Gilbert, Crowley & Hicklin, Fellows Morton & Clayton, the employers of canal workers remain shadowy figures. Men once wealthy and important have left little beyond their names to prove their passing.

James Sutton and his father between them handled much of the Manchester–Gainsborough traffic in the first half of the nineteenth century. George Jackson, another long-established carrier traded mainly between Manchester and Hull. James Shipton was an important operator based in the Midlands, and there were many more. The character of these men eludes us. Substantial individuals though they no doubt were, they remain ephemeral today.

GOODS DAILY FORWARDED BY

SHIPTONS AND CO.'S
LICENSED FLY BOATS,

TO AND FROM

LONDON, LIVERPOOL, MANCHESTER,
BIRMINGHAM, WOLVERHAMPTON,
PRESTON BROOK,

THE POTTERIES, CHESTER, WREXHAM, AND ALL PARTS OF THE NORTH.
BILSTON AND DUDLEY.
THE STAFFORDSHIRE IRON WORKS, AND ALL INTERMEDIATE PLACES.
Shardlow, Derby, Gainsborough, and Hull.

PLEASE TO CONSIGN ALL GOODS FROM

LONDON.	ISAAC SOWTER, 27, Wharf, City Basin —Receiving-house, White Horse, Cripplegate
Manchester.	SAMUEL WAINWRIGHT, Ashton Canal Wharf, Piccadilly
Liverpool.	ROBERT DICKINSON, Duke's Dock
Preston Brook,	GEORGE MILLER, Duke's Wharf
Potteries,	GEORGE GREEN, Canal Company's Wharfs
Chester and Wrexham.	SARAH RUTTER, Waggon Warehouse
Hull,	BROWN and BELL, High-street
Gainsborough,	FLOWER and SON
Shardlow and Derby,	SUTTON and Co.; and SORESBY and FLACK
Dudley,	Dudley-port Wharf
Gloucester,	BROWN and Co., Ship Basin
Bristol.	BROWN and Co., Head of Quay
Wolverhampton,	Albion Wharf, Horseley-fields
Birmingham,	Albion Wharf, Broad-street.

☞ *Goods forwarded to and from the West of England and South Wales.*

Fig 12 Shipton & Co, Carriers, 1832 (*Staffordshire County Record Office*)

144

The occasional person stands out; a distinctive manager brings something of a human face to otherwise anonymous concerns. There was John Houghton, 'Clerk to the Company of Proprietors of the Birmingham Canal Navigations in whose service nearly 50 years of his life were employed with sound judgement, indefatigable zeal, inflexible integrity and entire devotedness to promote the interests of the extensive undertakings';[3] Joseph Baxendale, manager, partner and dynamo of Pickfords in the first half of the nineteenth century; Thomas Hales of the Shropshire Union in the second half, along with contemporaries like Edward Pamphilon of the North Staffs, de Salis, Frederick Morton and Joshua Fellows of Fellows, Morton & Clayton; Leslie Morton of the Grand Union and Willow Wren in this century. But for the most part they all remain rather indistinct, disembodied individuals—names in newspapers, directories, canal company minutes.

One canal employer does come down through history as a three-dimensional figure. The achievement and eccentricity of the Duke of Bridgewater ensured that his life and character were fully documented; with the mystery of his love for the beautiful Duchess of Hamilton adding a certain spice to his rich personality.

A sickly, backward and tortured child, bruised by love in early manhood, burdened with colossal debt, the Duke grew into a courageous, stubborn and hard individual in maturer years—'his nature had certainly more of the oak than the flower in its composition'. His house and garden at Worsley were devoid of any sort of ornamentation and vegetation. A well meaning servant did once plant some flowers to brighten up the austere landscape, but their beauty was short-lived. On discovering them the Duke scythed off the heads with his cane and ordered them to be rooted up. There was no 'utility' at the heels of flowers. In his business dealings he was equally ruthless.

In later life, in contrast to the wispiness of his youth, he became large and unwieldy. He was careless about his clothes which were always cheap, brown and invariably soiled. He hated poultry and other 'white meats', drank little wine (after a lifetime's addiction to port) and he smoked considerably—'more than he talked'. Either he was obsessed with the weather or he may have had a weak bladder—'rushing out every five minutes to look at the barometer'. He was also, according to his sister-in-law, burdened with gout, a stomach disorder and irreligion. Lady Gower suspected too that he rarely washed and, she added, 'he Swears!'.

He had become something of a figure of fun to some of his aristocratic contemporaries, as he had been ridiculed for his wild scheme to carry water across water at Barton thirty-odd years before. The fact that he declined to fill the position expected of an English duke, preferring the company of his boatmen and canal workers, his miners and labourers to that of London society, tainted him as being something of a queer fish. His contact with his workers was frequent and familiar. In the vast organization that he came to control he knew many of them by name. For, despite his undoubted power and authority, beneath the somewhat rough, dour and untidy exterior there beat a kind heart.

One day the Duke spotted a workman arriving late for work (he kept a detailed eye upon his affairs). When questioned the labourer explained that during the night his wife had had the misfortune to have twins.

'Aye well, we have to have what the good Lord sends us,' said the Duke philosophically.

'Ah notice he sends all t'babies to our house and all t'brass to yores,' retorted the man, whereupon the Duke gave him a guinea.

Contemporaries often commented on the 'humanity and liberality' of 'that great personage in the treatment of the whole of his work force' and not least 'in making provision for his servants whom age or accident in his works had rendered unfit for service'. He paid good wages, built houses which he let at low rents, kept an eye on the price of provisions sold by local shopkeepers, paid doctors' bills, supported sick clubs and generally gave every care to the physical, moral and spiritual welfare of those who laboured on his behalf. His Grace the Duke of Bridgewater added a new dimension to the meaning of 'aristocratic paternalism'. No employer had a more loyal band of workers in return. Even many years after his death they still remembered him with 'affection and reverence', the more so perhaps since his successor at Worsley was not cast in the same mould.

We shall never be certain if it was the fickleness of an Irish beauty that turned the Duke from Society and women to the needs of his estates and his workers. If it were we should be grateful to her. It is certain that no family man would have pressed on with the risky ventures that he brought to success—at one time he was reduced to sending his agents around the estate begging farmers for loans to complete the canal to Runcorn. Whatever his foibles the Duke *was* respected because he was successful. When it became clear that his waterway gamble was not only of great benefit to the nation, but was on the way to making him a very wealthy man, he became something of a presence that permeated through the emerging canal world. For the most part it was a benevolent presence and canal companies generally imitated, among other things, his admirable labour relations. They became good employers by the standards of the time, and in many ways remained so.[4]

The Duke's main rival in the Liverpool to Manchester carrying trade, the Old Quay Company, followed his example. Their flatmen, for instance, were well looked after. It was not altogether humanitarianism which brought such concern for the work force. Flatmen fulfilled a vital role in the business as much as in the economic life of Lancashire and Cheshire. The employers knew it and so did the men. Not only were their demands often met, but there was continuing concern for their welfare. In 1832, when trade was slow, the Old Quay was reluctant to dismiss able and trustworthy flatmen, but preferred to find them jobs as temporary porters—sacking some of the porters instead. True, the porters were probably not too happy about the plan and there was self-interest in the company's decision because competent flatmen would be on hand for any 'extraordinary pushes in business', but it was felt that 'porters could more easily find employment than discharged flatmen'.

The same company was the first, in 1834, in granting a respite from the Sunday labour which had infiltrated the canal world. The men were paid (fortnightly) on the Friday night, when most firms paid on Saturday. This was reckoned to increase the value of the wage since they could make their purchases more advantageously. The company went to the trouble and expense of furthering the educational and spiritual needs of the flatmen and their families in the form of schools and encouragement to church attendance.

Nor were such old servants as could no longer work, through advancing senility, cast off. In 1837 the Old Quay was employing flatmen who were 'very old servants and infirm, merely having the charge of such Flats as are tied up and do any other work they are able'.[5]

It was the same story on most canals where the canal company carried in its own boats. The land staff were equally well cared for. On the Barnsley Canal in 1832 it was ordered that 'Ten Pounds be given to John Jackson one of the Company's Lockkeepers who from long continued Sickness in his Family has incurred great expenses in medical assistance'. On the Weaver there was an old established rule 'for preferring old and deserving servants and their descendants to places under the Navigation'. Dependants were looked after. Mrs Butterfield, widow of a Leeds porter, was granted one guinea by the Aire & Calder in 1790 when she was in 'distressed circumstances'; as was the widow of a lock-keeper killed accidentally on the Derby Canal in 1847—granted £5 5s a week. Pensions were the rule rather than the exception.

Of course millions of tons were handled, not by the canal companies, but by independent operators who employed hundreds of land staff and boatmen. What was it like to work for them?

Apart from the Duke of Bridgewater, who was rather special, it was very rare that any observer saw fit to draw a picture of such men in the round—with one exception. He was John Hargreaves, whose ancestors were carriers in the days of the 'pack saddle'. Along with Pickfords they came to form, on land and water, the two main carrying concerns of England and Scotland long before other noted carriers entered the field. John Hargreaves directed the fortunes of the firm during much of the Canal Age. Pennington remembered him as he was in the 1830s.

The artist who first gave a sketch of 'John Bull' as that worthy gentleman has often appeared in *Punch* must have had Mr Hargreaves in mind when he drew the character, the likeness being perfect.

I, my brothers and sisters, when children had a great reverence for the imposing looking gentleman and gazed upon him as we would on a king; with his large head, bulky body, broad red face, prominent nose, mutton-chop sandy whiskers, dark red curly hair, 'broad gauge' legs, pondrous and swinging walk, knee breeches, top shiny boots, massive gold snuff box, heavy gold chain with giant seals, hanging from his fob, fine silk broad brimmed hat, immense broadcloth black 'top' coat, with pockets of capacious dimensions filled with papers; a grand English gentleman. . . .

He was not a man to be treated lightly. He once had a quarrel with a toll-gate man.

'What are you, sir?' queried the collector contemptuously. 'You are only a common carrier.'

'I am an uncommon carrier,' thundered back Mr Hargreaves. 'I carry further than any man in England.'

For all that, he was, like the Duke of Bridgewater, a man with the common touch. He knew his men intimately and always spoke to them in a familiar style as 'Well, John' or 'Well, Thomas'.

One suspects that there was about John Hargreaves much that was typical of many other carriers and canal men in the Canal Age —cast in an heroic mould, larger than life, dynamic, 'trouble shooters' (and there were plenty of troubles to shoot in the canal world—the weather, the state of trade, the men, the customers). The diary of G. R. Bird, the Birmingham carrier, gives a hint of some of the human difficulties when 'Thos. Derby of the firm of Derby Brothers called on me at our office on Wednesday Evening 8-o'-clock 14 September 1825 and insulted me. Turned him and his friend out of the office'.[6]

They loved to be in the thick of things, like the Duke of Bridge-water, keeping a close eye on their affairs. Hargreaves visited his out-stations between Manchester and Edinburgh every three months, collecting the larger freight accounts himself. If he travelled by stage-coach he often drove it. Baxendale too was for ever on the go, visiting Pickfords' stations throughout the country.

They were hearty drinkers and eaters. Bird was another carrier with the gout and he dined often with other Midland carriers 'Worthington, Crockett, Crowley, Robinson and Smith Dined with me this day at five'; 'I Dine with the members of the Bean club this day at the Royal Hotel'; 'Mr Baxendale Mr Ames Mr Fleck Mr Worthington Mr Crockett Mr Crowley very Pleasant Dined with me this day 19 October 1826', which tends to indicate that competitors though they might be, they were all good friends with one another. They had the capacity to handle men who could be difficult. Baxendale described his boatmen as being 'very manageable'.

Joseph Baxendale was, in fact, the son of a Lancaster physician. He went into the cotton trade on leaving school and was later sent to London to represent his firm. He abandoned cotton after a disagreement with his employers and joined Pickfords who were in desperate straits at that time (1817). He put money into the business and took a lively interest in its management. 'Baxendale was energetic cheerful and witty. He ruled his employees with an iron hand, but managed at the same time to remain popular with them. He was quick to reward initiative and reward young people.'[7]

The employees of such men generally responded with their loyalty. John Lea mentioned that '. . . when riots occurred in the North some time ago [probably 1842] a commercial gentleman stated that a considerable number of boatmen . . . so far from joining the disaffected, manifested a decided determination to defend their masters' property, if assailed'.[8] A common feature of canal workers was that many of them worked for the same employer for many years, often for all their working lives. We read in the *Birmingham Gazette* of 22 November 1824, 'Died on Thursday last, after a very short illness, in the 53rd year of his age William Ambrose an honest and faithful servant having been in the employ of Mr G. R. Bird upwards of twenty years as captain of one of his boats'. Captain Randle was a boatman with Pickfords for forty years and then the connection was only broken because they ceased canal trading in 1848.[9]

If the heroic characters of the Canal Age tended to be replaced by more sedate gentlemen like Thomas Hales, as the whole of the economy became less individually dynamic and more corporate, the traditions of benevolence and loyalty of the canal world continued. John Brydone explained in 1889 how Mr Hales had 'tried to benefit the canal-boat people, in whom he has always taken the most lively interest and I have to acknowledge his hearty cooperation in all matters connected with the company's large fleet of boats'.[10] Boatmen were loaned money to see them through troubled times—sickness, injury, the death of a horse. It became more general to grant pensions to watermen, as on 29 October 1884 with

John Carman of the Flat 'Richard' who had been in the employ of the Company 50 years, also of William Cox of the boat 'Ella' who had worked for the Company for 40 years and is now 79 years of age and is incapable of working his boat. It was agreed to allow a superannuation of 5s a week in each case.

The Birmingham Canal Navigations Committee was 'mindful of and is giving assistance to the dependants of the Company's servants who have joined the colours' in February 1915.

The Bridgewater tradition continued. A visitor to the Grand Junction and Regent's Canals in 1925 found 'no more loyal band of workers'. This was 'largely the result of the way in which the companies look after their employees'. John Bliss, the manager, himself with the company for forty-eight years, 'was obviously on the most friendly terms with every employee met with, and the happiest relations appeared to exist between all ranks'.[11] The same paternalism characterised many of the independent carrying companies. Mr Lewis, in 1920, knew 'some of them take a very great interest in their employees. For instance the General Manager [Mr Danks] of the largest carriers [Severn Canal Carrying Company Co] is looked upon as a kind of father to these boatmen'.[12] The same tradition continued down to the final days. John Saxon remembers how in the 1950s he gave a lift to a ship's lifeboat belonging to some students by hoisting it on to his coal-laden narrow boat.

> By the time I had reached Braunston the boatman's telegraph had been at work and my boss, Mr David Campbell [of Samuel Barlow's], was standing on the towpath. . . . Mr Campbell started shouting at me as I went past and told me I would be sacked when I got back, but I waved to him and smiled to myself, because I knew that he did not mean it.
>
> David Campbell was a good gaffer to work for but, most of all, he was a good friend of the boat people. He was a fair and honest man and I feel proud to have worked for him. He made me captain of a pair of boats at the age of nineteen, and helped me through some rough times.[13]

Canal workers had perhaps had to mind their Ps and Qs more in the nineteenth century. On the Monmouthshire Canal a minute of 27 April 1801 ordered that 'two of the Company's lock keepers be immediately Discharged in consequence of their being active in the late Riots at Pontpool'. And there was another side to the coin of benevolence if a man fell from grace—the possible loss of his hoped-for pension or his home, if not his job. The Duchess of Atholl drew attention to the

> . . . sword of Damocles . . . over every canal boat man who has no house in the event of his losing his employment? If a man falls out with his employer or loses his health, or is unable to continue his work for any other reason, think of his fate. It means not only loss of employment, but loss of his home, and that is the fate which descended on no fewer than 129 families a few years ago when a canal boat company dismissed all its workers. There had been some trouble with the men, and the result was that they were all dismissed. Some 129 families were affected of whom 72 were without home.[14]

The 'Gentlemen's Agreement' between the major carriers, which operated after World War II, effectively made the boatmen slaves to one employer because, in theory, no other operator would accept a boatman from another company unless he had been sacked, or it was clear that he was going on land and would otherwise be lost to the industry. True the scheme did not always work out in practice, as when boatmen were in short supply in recent years. Employers cheated the system and exchanged vitriolic letters with each other in consequence. Boatmen, whether they knew about their bondage or not, did find ways to dodge off to richer pastures.

And there *were* some bad, hard employers. John Crowley's remark in 1841 that 'I do not apprehend the Sunday is a necessary Time for resting having that time from Labour for the Men every Night', shows no great concern for the welfare of Crowley & Hicklin's boatmen and adds some substance to the Reverend Davies' criticism. There was the boat owner who fined his men ten shillings or dismissed them if he found that they had rested on a Sunday.[15] By all accounts it was no fun to work for Robert Bradshaw, the superintendent of the Bridgewater Trust from 1803, a wild-tempered man more concerned with profit than humanity. Worsley became 'a God-forgotten place, its inhabitants much addicted to drink and rude sports, their morals being deplorably low', a situation which continued until 1834 when a new superintendent and, more especially, Lord Francis Egerton and his wife came to cast a more benevolent eye upon the undertaking. They carried on, if not in the style, then in the spirit of their noble ancestor.[16]

Some boats—especially those carrying obnoxious cargoes—were a disgrace to their owners and were an obvious mark of the lack of concern of the employers for their boatmen. In 1925 Dr Dearden inferred that boat owners were more concerned with their pockets than the health and well-being of the boat people. But of course by then the economic climate had turned against the employers as much as against the men.

The canal companies and the larger carriers were by and large good employers, but there were many small firms involved in canal trading, including industrial firms carrying their own produce or boating concerns owning a handful of vessels. Among these there were indeed employers who fully deserved to be castigated. During the Canal Age, for instance, there were some small operators who would offer to carry at rates so low that no one else could afford to compete. This they could do by cutting numerous corners, including the paying of very low wages. It was tacitly understood that these wages would be made up by pilfering. However, it was by no means always the case that small meant bad. One owner of a few boats insisted that his men rest on a Sunday and paid £2 10s 0d a week for extra horses to ensure their Sabbath repose.[17] Still, in 1909, Mr Llewellyn complained that the 'only class that does not seem to realise the necessity for improvement is the small boat owner'.

Returning to the 'great hinge' of the 'wages question' there has always been much controversy as to whether the boat people were well paid or the opposite. To assess the earnings of the watermen is a very difficult business because so much depended upon the type of goods carried, the size of the vessel and the amount available to be carried. Few statistics on wages have survived and where they have it is not always clear exactly what they represent—the horse and other incidentals often having to be taken into account.

It is clear, however, that some very large sums came into the watermen's hands by the standards of the time, especially to the men working the larger craft. And the reporter of the *Standard* chided one narrow-boat captain, on being told that he earned

£2 10s od per week for himself and family in 1877, 'They are excellent wages ...; hundreds of clerks up in London make less, and few artisans more ....'.

Captain Jonah retorted that they might be considered good wages 'by any one as didn't know all the expenses the boatmen were at. I've lost two horses only lately, and I give eleven pounds for that there 'orse. Where's I to get another eleven pounds if I looses that 'un?'

But not every boatman lost two horses and the evidence of many observers was that the boat people lived extremely well. Captain Jonah with whom 'things could not be wuss' dined in the evening on '... a tempting knuckle of ham, a shapely piece of corned beef, fat and lean and admirably blended, a crusty loaf of fresh baked bread, a dish of pickled onions and cucumber, and a goodly can of ale. In the morning there was an unlimited supply of milk, fresh from the cow, for the children, tea and bread for the skipper, his wife and guest ...'

In the early 1920s the daily menu attributed by a London firm of canal carriers to their boatmen was:

4.30 am   Tea with meat sandwiches, or a plate of meat.
7.00 am   (breakfast) Bacon.
10.30 am   A 'reaver' of bread, meat and bottled beer.
Noon   Dinner with meat.
5.00 pm   Early tea with meat left from dinner.
7.00 pm   Tea with more cooked meat.
10.00 pm   Supper with more meat.[18]

The *Standard* reporter concluded that he agreed with the clergyman who insisted that the men as a rule ate well, drank well and smoked well—they earned ample to keep themselves in comfort 'if', the clergyman added darkly, 'the boatmen would only keep out of the beershop'.

Not all the boat people drank, however, by any means, and as a general rule the boat people were not poor. They may have been relatively poorer in the sense that they had, by the later nineteenth century, to work longer hours to earn the same amount of money, and in the sense that the family was in more cases taking over the labour of working the boat. They may have been poorly paid when the large number of hours worked is taken into account—

hourly rates as compared with other workers are almost impossible to work out—but they were not poor. The finances of the boaters did suffer more from the 1890s, but the Rev Hills could still comment in 1920, 'We do not find a great deal of poverty'.

'They live very well,' observed a Runcorn inspector, 'that is one thing that they do.'[19]

There *was* some poverty on the canals. There were people who, for various reasons, did not earn enough. There were those rendered poor temporarily by circumstances such as a strike by others; periods of slack trade; or during bad weather conditions.

Frost was the boat people's greatest enemy. From the earliest times boatmen were not paid during frost. Then, from the middle of the nineteenth century, the larger companies began to make advances against future earnings and from the beginning of this century half pay became the rule. At the onset of frost companies would 'shepherd them up to the nearest depot . . . take the horses off them and put them in the stables, gather the men together and then begin to allow them so much a week . . .', Mr Jones, the manager of FMC, explained in 1920.[20] But many boatmen still got paid nothing and even company boatmen could get frozen in at such isolated places that they were soon in dire straits. During the severe weather in 1928 one family got so short of food that the baby was constantly crying for bread.

'I'll get baby bread, mammy,' said the little daughter of eight.

She went to beg at a house near the side of the canal, but was attacked by a yard dog and badly bitten on the wrist and thigh.

There were many similar families scattered all over the canals who suffered semi-starvation during that frost and there always had been. Those who received nothing from their employers sometimes tried to get poor relief or unemployment benefit, but they often found that the officials ruled that they were not out of employment and gave them nothing. Since many had no fixed parish they were frequently refused poor relief as well, or at best offered a place in the workhouse.

A woman and her two daughters were found starving in a boat tied up in the Wolverhampton basin in 1921. The captain was in hospital suffering from pneumonia. Not knowing how to apply for the National Insurance money, they had made application to the Poor Law Authorities for relief, and had been offered an order for admission, which they refused. The NSPCC inspector saw the Relieving Officer and the Clerk to the Guardians, explaining that if the family left the boat, their only home, they would lose it, and probably be inmates of the workhouse for an indefinite period. He was able to get them a grant of 18s a week, which tided them over their time of trouble until the boatman was able to work again.[21] Such cases did not always end so happily.

Canal companies and carriers (often the two were the same from the mid-nineteenth century) were not bad employers and in many ways had been model employers. It was in the form of the aristocratic paternalism of the eighteenth century (which merged into the industrial paternalism of the Arkwrights, the Peels and the Owens). Such paternalism had been one of the better aspects of eighteenth and early nineteenth century life when it worked well. The lord, the squire or the industrialist accepted the responsibility of looking after the people he felt to be under his care as best he could, according to his lights. In turn the workman gave his labour and very often his loyalty to the master. But it was a haphazard system. There were good masters and bad and there was little redress against the bad. It was very much what the master thought was good for you. Often a once-benevolent company or carrier was by-passed by time; induced to cut corners because of economics.

The law must ensure a minimum benevolence for all men, women and children, regardless of economic conditions and the law was late in coming to the canals. The first Factory Act came in 1802, but it was not until 1877 and 1884 that canal women and children received the attention of the legislature, and this did not take them out of the boats.

By the 1920s the paternalism which had, with all its flaws, served the canal industry so well was out of date. A state of affairs had gradually emerged which could no longer be tolerated, especially in the changed economic climate of the post-war years. Both the canal staff and the boat people became equally restless and turned belatedly to trade unionism for help. The TGWU in taking the matter in hand, commented on the 'very bad conditions and low rate of wages under which the workers are employed'. Some of the things which they had to suffer could 'be described only as scandalous'.[22]

10
Help and Self Help

In 1923 Fellows Morton & Clayton, the largest boat-owning company, tried to push down rates by 4d a ton, or $6\frac{1}{2}$ per cent. Trade was particularly depressed and the old evil of waiting around for loads with little or no payment for days on end fell very heavily upon the boat people. The overall effect, they claimed, would be a reduction from an already thin weekly earning of £1 down to 15s.

'Before the war we might have managed,' said one boatman, 'but we are getting pinched. We've never struck before but we can't stand any more Irishman's rises.'[1]

To a man (and woman) the boat people struck and for twelve weeks not one of the company's boats moved, nor did the large fleets of two other important companies. 'The solidarity among the men and women concerned is remarkable and their determination to carry on the dispute . . . is unwavering', their representative claimed.

It was the same story again in 1927 when the Severn & Canal Carrying Company tried to reduce the rates drastically (by up to 30 per cent) whereupon 'every one of the boatmen employed by the Company . . . ceased work, and they remained loyal to each other throughout the stoppage'.

The strikers in both disputes were not unmindful of their employers' position in those difficult years. 'The men acknowledged all through that the Company was not in a rosy position. Very few concerns connected with canal transport are just now', but they felt that they were being asked 'to make too big a contribution'.

In the end, both strikes ended with the men 'winning' less of a reduction (5 per cent instead of $6\frac{1}{2}$ per cent in 1923).

It was felt at the time that it was union interference which had precipitated the 1923 strike. The *Manchester Guardian* reported that it was due 'to an accident that they now belong to the Transport Workers Union'. Fellows Morton also blamed union activity, especially one Fred Potter, the Brentford delegate. The suggestion was that he had corrupted the boat people. 'They are men who have been in the employment... of the Company for many years. Their sons and grandsons were also ...'. If 'the activities of ... [Fred Potter] could be restrained', they claimed, 'there would be no difficulty in coming to terms with the men'.[2]

It is true that the union did give the boatmen greater bargaining power through stronger organisation, but it is clear that they were behind the union to a man (and woman), with or without Fred Potter. The suggestion put out that this was the first strike of inland watermen has also left a false impression. It *was* the first strike of Fellows Morton's workers in over forty years of the company's existence, which is indeed a demonstration of the good relations generally existing between employers and men in that company, and there were many others like it. But the suggestion that union activity changed this blissful picture is wrong, since canal workers, benevolent employers or not, had never been afraid to withdraw their labour when squeezed by hard times.

A report of the 1923 strike is in marked contrast to one of a hundred years before. 'During the strike period the behaviour of the people was exemplary. The happiest relations existed between them and the [Birmingham] police.'[3] One Fellows Morton man is rumoured to have got a ducking at Braunston and there was some hard talk at Brentford, but nothing to compare with the events of 1822 when Pickfords' boatmen had cut towing ropes, hurled horses and blacklegs into the water, thrown stones and done battle with the police during their strike at the City Road basin.[4]

Nor was this the first withdrawal of labour. As early as 1792 there is a record of an important strike by the salt flatmen. Then there was the famous strike of 1796 which began.

> ... in Consequence of a letter of August 11th with the signature of 'the Flatmen' [of the Old Quay Company] appearing to be wrote from the Seven Stars Warrington ... requiring an Advance of Wages and threatening to tie up the Vessels and it appearing ...

that nearly the whole of the Flatmen are now out of Employ for an Advance of Wages.[5]

They were successful and the formula thrashed out then survived, with some variations, for many years—until 1840 in fact when the men again 'turned out' for an advance of wages. Even in those days there were 'reds under the bed', for those 'wicked Socialist Missionaries' were coming from Manchester and Liverpool to spread their 'abominable doctrines' among the flatmen.

Nor was it merely during the turbulent years of the Industrial Revolution that unrest could erupt among the watermen. The Shropshire Union Company was still resisting trade union interference into its affairs as late as 1910. 'Mr Hales stated he had received an application from Mr Ben Tillett chairman of the Boatmen and Dockers Union, to know the rates of wages paid to the Company's men and that he did not propose to reply to the letter. Approved.' This did not prevent the boatmen and porters going on strike in 1911 as the boatmen and flatmen had done several times in the second half of the nineteenth century.[6]

In June alone in 1892 there were three strikes—by the bargemen on the Regent's and the Rochdale Canals and by those on the River Medway, followed by a violent dispute of the Salt Union's men on the River Weaver in August which resulted in damaged property, reinforcement of the police by the military and a threat from the Liverpool dockers to come out in sympathy. The strike was finally settled through the intervention of the Bishop of Chester.[7]

Trade unions and legislation and many other of the benefits which came to improve the lot of the working classes were late in coming to the canals. For many years the canal people—the boaters—were very much on their own. Benevolent employers some may have had, but the hazards of the trade; the nature of the work which cut them off from others on land; the fact that the world seemed often set against them—being variously abused as 'gypsies', 'boaties' and 'keelies'—made them an independent, self-reliant and inward-looking race. Hence there grew up a strong tradition of self-help and an acting together in the face of adversity which lasted until their demise in recent years.

One of the first examples of this took place as early as 1774,

GRAND JUNCTION CANAL CO.

CAUTION TO BOATMEN.

At the Clerkenwell Police Court, on Monday, the 23rd May, 1864, **BENJAMIN WILSON** was convicted of intimidating and compelling the hands to quit the boat "Fleetwood," and sentenced to One Month's Imprisonment, with Hard Labour; and, at the same Court, on Monday, May 30th, **JOHN MUSSON** was brought up on remand, and convicted of assaulting and compelling a Boatman to leave the boat "Grays," and sentenced to Two Months' Imprisonment, with Hard Labour, in the House of Correction.

NOTICE IS HEREBY GIVEN,

That the Hands who joined **WILSON** and **MUSSON** in the above outrages are strictly prohibited from working with the Boats again, and that any Steerer employing or harbouring any of them after this Notice will be instantly discharged.

CITY ROAD BASIN,
2nd June, 1864.

By Order.

Waterlow and Sons, Printers, Carpenters' Hall, London Wall.

Fig 13 Caution to Boatmen; 'shop stewards' get short shrift in 1864 (*Waterways Museum*)

again during a severe frost, when boatmen on the Oxford and Coventry canals were made destitute because they could no longer work. Eighteen of them banded together to load a waggon with coal at Bedworth in Warwickshire which they proceeded to draw through the snow to London to present to the King. The unusual spectacle of men pulling a waggon drew numerous onlookers and considerable sums of money were collected from every place they passed through. When they arrived at St James the King sent them twenty guineas without taking the coal. This they were allowed to dispose of as they liked.[8]

Similarly, in this century, despite internal squabblings, the boat people rallied to help one another as in the case of the boatman who lost two sons by drowning in the space of eight months in 1937. He was unable to raise sufficient money for the burial of the second lad, but John Blacker, another boatman, learned of his plight and immediately organised a collection, which raised enough money for the funeral and to provide mourning for the boy's three sisters and brother. In 1910 the boat people had subscribed £5 amongst themselves to defray the expenses of the funeral of George Blakemore (the supposed orphan).[9]

There were organised forms of self-help among the watermen, like the friendly societies formed by the flatmen and keelmen, by the boatmen of the Stroudwater Navigation, and there were the boat-building clubs of the Birmingham boatmen, but for the most part, and especially among the narrow-boat people, it was more a case of helping a neighbour in need—shoving off a grounded boat, helping each other through childbirth, lending a hand to a boat where some one was ill, and so on.

For all that there was this feeling of solidarity, it was a hard life on the canals—one which suited the strong and able. It was not really a place for the weak and the sick—the widows and orphans and those who could not always help themselves. There were times too when the distress was so widespread, as during a severe frost, that the canal world was laid destitute and powerless to help itself. Because of their isolation and nomadism it was much less possible for the water people to turn to the instruments which helped others on land—the Poor Law and local charities.

The established Church seemed little concerned with the peculiarities and problems of the waterway people in the Canal Age, apart from occasional broadsides against their sinful ways. One can understand some of the reticence of the clergy if they had heard of the treatment meted out to the Vicar of Mexborough.

> Whereas on Monday the 31st day of December 1821 Joseph Mason of Doncaster, waterman, did conduct himself in a most violent and outrageous manner towards the resident Minister of Mexbro' using language too horrible to be repeated, and even threatening to take away his life; likewise James Pool, Potseller, Richard Harrup and Joseph Scholey, watermen with others, all of Mexbro'... did aid abet, and encourage...Joseph Mason, by shouts and threats, so as to put the Reverend Gentleman in fear of his personal safety.[10]

Still, decent flatmen found it difficult to get into the Weaver churches. Boat people were generally unwelcome.

Some few clergymen with parishes along the banks of the canal began in the 1830s to occupy themselves with the boat people: the Reverend Davies at Worcester and Runcorn; the Reverend Wade at Kidsgrove; the Reverend Hollins at Gloucester. The Paddington Society for Promoting Christian Knowledge (of unknown denomination) functioned for a time (1829-32) among the boatmen. Floating chapels mushroomed after the scandal of Christina Collins. The Weaver Trustees actually paid for the building of three churches for the flatmen. And in other ways there were those engaged 'in plucking a little encouraging fruit from this plant, which for so long has been allowed to run wild...'.

In to the spiritual vacuum generally left by the Church stepped the nonconformists, the Methodists in particular, and down to recent times this nonconformist tradition lingered among the flatmen of the Mersey and the keelmen of Yorkshire. Such faiths as that of Primitive Methodism had a special appeal to those who felt themselves outcasts from society.

The narrow boatmen were less religious, although there were some staunch Christians among them. More boat people did come to appreciate the love of God rather than his wrath from the 1870s, as the Seamen and Boatmen's Friend Society expanded its mission work much more into inland waterways. These missionaries criticized less and helped more with the peculiar needs of the waterway people, especially during hard times. 'The watermen,

Fig 14 Entertainment at the Boatmen's Hall, Birmingham (*British Library*)

even the rudest roughest boatmen, can appreciate kindly intended effort, and by the grace of God, even his heart can be softened and changed,' wrote the Reverend Hollins. And it was exactly this sort of kindly friendliness which the boat people came to appreciate from the missionaries of the Society. The report of the Birmingham branch in 1894 gives some indication of the work done for the boat people.

The coffee and reading rooms have been visited by upwards of 10,000 persons . . . and 202 letters have been written . . . free of charge . . . upwards of 11,000 homes, boats and toll offices have been visited by the missionaries at Birmingham and Hednesford.

Between 200 and 300 boats were visited weekly. One boatman told a visiting missionary at Dudley Port in 1898, 'Well this is a great change to what it was a few years back, you never had anyone to visit you, or read to you then, and there was fighting and swearing on the canals but you don't see so much of that now'.[11] It was generally agreed that the boat people were a much improved race by 1900 after twenty-five years or so of hard effort by the Society.

There were other and perhaps still more important measures afoot. There is no doubt that the greatest uplift for the boat people came from the work of George Smith, who thrust before the public details of the unsavoury side of canal life. He was a peculiar creature, hated by most boat people, for he did many of them a great disservice in the sense that he confirmed public prejudices about the boaters that were not true in the majority of cases. Still, though he was unfair and untruthful about many details of the life style of most boat people, there *were* many unpleasant aspects of waterway life and he did succeed in getting laws passed in 1877 and 1884 which, despite imperfections, led to much improvement in living and working conditions. He himself would have liked to have seen to the enforcement of the Canal Boats Acts, but he was to be disappointed. John Brydone was appointed chief inspector instead. Smith, despite his philanthropy and concern for the boat children, seems to have had little real sympathy with the waterway folk, whereas Brydone quickly tuned in to their way of life. He was efficient without being officious. He was 'an able, quiet, steady thoughtful man, able to see what is required, firm to carry the same into effect'. His successor discovered that he was 'a man of whom one hears without exception, nothing but good', and to him must go much of the credit for raising those on the canals who were of a 'low and debased standard' to become 'honest useful members of society'.[12]

The canal boat inspectors (usually local sanitary inspectors) who followed the missionaries onto the towpath were, for the most part, welcomed with equal courtesy. There were the odd incidents early on, when one or two inspectors tested the depth of the canal, and there was the case where the Leigh inspector in 1903 had to write of a Manchester boat *Victoria*, 'Captain refused to produce certificate and used foul language—wrote owner re same'. Generally the inspectors approached the job in the spirit of their chief and came to be regarded as real friends by the boat people. Owen Llewellyn, the second and last chief canal boats' inspector, came to be as enamoured of the boat people as Brydone had been. He, and many missionaries too, came to defend them against attack; so much so that they often came under criticism themselves. Perhaps it is true to say that they had become so involved with the boat people that they sometimes defended that which was really indefensible—such as having children on boats.

Fig 15 John I. Watts, champion of the boat children (*Director, NSPCC*)

One area of criticism came from the National Society for the Prevention of Cruelty to Children which entered the field in the 1890s and devoted forty years of serious effort to improving the condition of the canal-boat children and to getting them educated. The great champion of these children was John I. Watts, for many years secretary of the NSPCC's Northwich branch and a member of the Central Executive Committee. He drew public attention to the peculiar problems of these children. In 1919 he personally paid for a special Canal Boats Inspector to be appointed. Mr Hackett duly came on to the towpath and did much to reduce the labour and improve the condition of young children in the 1920s and 1930s. The mere fact that such an inspector existed did much to ameliorate their lot. Lock-keepers, on seeing children being asked to do tasks they ought not to do, would quietly say to the parents, 'The Children's Inspector is about'.

The main aim of the NSPCC was to get the children out of the boats altogether and for thirty years it strove to get a Bill before Parliament, finally succeeding with the Canal Boats Bill of 1929.

Plate 29 Sister Mary Ward attends to boat people in her surgery at Stoke Bruerne, 1950 (*Waterways Museum*)

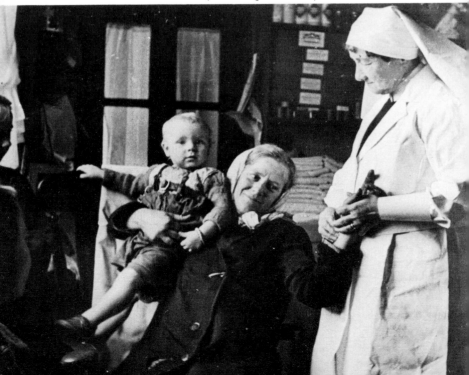

Though there was a large majority for it in the House, it was talked out after a determined opposition led by Earl Winterton and Sir Herbert Nield, a director of the Grand Union Canal Company. None the less, the publicity which surrounded the Bill did lead to further improvement in the condition of the children.

In the post-war twilight years of commercial carrying the Salvation Army brought its own particular brand of cheer to the boat people in the form of Brigadier and Mrs Frederick Fielding with their fleet of two narrow boats *Salvo* and *Aster*. They too became good friends of the boat folk as they voyaged through the narrow canals, helping them with their sick animals, collecting and distributing clothing for the needy, visiting people in hospital, writing letters and helping at confinements, as well as holding Sunday school classes on board or at their base at Sutton Stop.

There were others, too, who, though it was often a part of their job, approached the boat people in a kindly way, accepting the constraints imposed by the nature of the boat people's life rather than railing against them. Many a boat child learned the rudiments of reading and writing from the dedicated and sympathetic teachers at mission schools, of which there were a fair number in the nineteenth century. Most teachers did not take kindly to boat children. Miss Selina Dix MBE, head teacher at a school in Coventry admitted, 'we always watch them right away because we do not like them mixing with our own children. We have had pilfering and many other things of that kind. . . . They are very careless about the language they use: I do not believe they know'.[13] Mrs Purvis liked them. She was one of the last teachers at the special school for boat children at Southall which closed when British Waterways ceased carrying in 1963.

'If the school had not closed I might never have retired,' said Mrs Purvis. 'I don't think I could have left them. I would not have missed the experience for anything.'

The state did finally, in 1952, step in with a solution to the education problem; one that many continental countries had first adopted over fifty years before. A hostel was opened for twenty-nine canal-boat children at Wood End Hall, Erdington, in Birmingham. From there they attended local schools and returned to the boats in the holidays. Suspicious of it at first the boat people soon came to appreciate its value. The children were less keen and

Plate 30 Missionaries at work among the Mersey flatmen in Canning Dock, Liverpool, 1900 (*British Library*)

never really adapted themselves to the constraints of living in a house . . . and other disciplines. 'You have to be in bed at six o'clock,' one boat child complained.

There were others who held the trust of the boat people—the woman who 'went about' as midwife in 1877; Nurse Jones at Brentford in the early years of this century; Dr Smith of Southall and Sister Mary Ward at Stoke Bruerne who both took a special interest in the welfare of the boaters in the 1940s and 1950s; Sister Hanson of the British Waterway's Board at Bulls Bridge in the closing years of carrying.

The waterway workers began to organize themselves for their own improvement on a more formal basis from the 1890s. It was mainly on the broad waterways at first and even there organization was difficult. The Watermen and Riverside Labourers Union founded in 1890 was an organization of keelmen, boatmen and general labourers based on Leeds. Membership increased considerably during a dispute in 1891. There were 'many of them who had never belonged to any organization in their lives before', but when

TELEPHONE :
ROADE 395

THE SURGERY,

STOKE BRUERNE,

TOWCESTER,

NORTHAMPTONSHIRE.

april 30 '1957.

monday 10·42 PM·

Dear Mr Campbell.

Request to report, Sam Higgins, Steerer,
had an accident to hand, thick steel wire, was
wrapped around blades, Sam tried to remove
the same, which caused a nasty wound, I stitched
wound, dressing of course, but as patient, had
lost rather a lot of blood — I naturally could
not use right hand, I said, bed for some hours.
therefore am afraid Boats will be somewhat
delayed, — although I said they could
continue journey, hence this note to you.

2.

Hope you o yours are well.

Yours truly,

Sister Mary.

(Mary E. W. d OBE)

Fig 16 Letter from Sister Mary Ward OBE, 'Consultant Sister
to long distance boatmen and families, British canals' (*David
Campbell*)

169

they had got the advance from the employers and the dispute was over some of them—'chiefly of the ignorant classes'—left it. Others waited to draw on the winter distress fund before they left. The president of the union complained, 'the [water] men did not really know what organisation is'.[14]

Unionism on the waterways did advance, but it was not really until the 1920s that the people of the narrow canals seriously embraced it. Then they got the whole power of the Transport and General Workers Union behind them. The canal people found two champions in the kindly Harry Gosling, president of the union and a former Minister of Transport, and the dynamic colossus Ernest Bevin, secretary of the whole union. 'Probably the section of the Union which requires the greatest organising effort for improvement so far as working conditions are concerned is the waterways group, with particular reference to canals', stated the *Record* in August 1921.

The union restated its interest after the strike of 1923 which it saw as a resounding success: 'We won recognition, we won arbitration and we won a revision of the employers' claims.'

'But that it is not the end,' the *Record* went on in December. 'The Union means to tackle the conditions of employment on the canals, and although it is bound to be a long and tedious job, with the solid support of the canal boatmen themselves, even that battle will be won.'

The canal workers seem generally to have remained loyal to the union through the difficult economic times of the inter-war years —in March 1924 it could record nearly 100 per cent membership both in the craft and among the maintenance staff. In May 1927, despite 'the flow of work being very uncertain and irregular . . . Union membership is good'.

The union in turn did have considerable success in resisting wage cuts and in actually improving wages and conditions during a difficult economic period and during years of falling prices. The *Record* of August 1929 reveals that a Grand Union Conciliation Board had been set up in February and had formalized agreements on wages and conditions for land staff on the Grand Union which shows that, although wages were not excessive, they were still well above the lowest paid in the working class. Craftsmen seem to have been worst off although some were paid more than the figures in

Table 1 indicate. The statistics almost certainly reflect a relative worsening of the position of the land staff as compared with their nineteenth-century predecessors.

Table 1

COMPARATIVE RATES OF PAY, 1929[15]

	Old Regent's Canal	Old Grand Junction	Warwick Canals Section	hour week
Lock-keepers	65s	54s	48s	48
Horse drivers	60s			48
Tradesmen (bricklayers carpenters etc)		60s	58s	48
Lengthsmen ⎫ Labourers ⎬		54s		48
Lengthsmen			48s	48
Tugmen (Islington)	81s			48

Agricultural labourers (England and Wales)	31s 8d
One Horse carters (UK)	52s 10d
Carpenters and Joiners (UK)	72s 3d
Labourers in local authority service (UK)	52s 5d

The union achieved a closed shop with the Midland and Coast Canal Carrying Company in 1931. The formation of the Grand Union Canal Carrying Company gave employment to many boatmen, the majority of whom were already 'organized'. Active steps were being taken to 'bring in the "nons" and secure 100 per cent organisation' in 1935. A Midland Canal Wages Board was set up and one of the first results was holidays with pay for boatmen.

It was, as the union had foreseen, all very hard going, but gradually in the 1930s wages improved; hours (mainly for land staff) were reduced; the union did much to force the recognition of women as employees; rates for waiting to unload (demurrage) were negotiated; compensation for other delays such as those caused by a canal breach were also agreed on.

The War brought considerable progress and in 1943 a National Joint Industrial Council for the inland waterways was set up, which looked at the industry as a whole. In May 1943 the first national agreement for canal workers was signed. This meant a levelling up of wages by various amounts and by the end of 1946 the union was able to get the first national minimum wage agreement. 'This to the canal worker was a tremendous step forward,' claimed the union, and it was something of a pinnacle of achievement too 'when we cast our minds back to the conditions of [waterway workers] . . . 25 years ago and compare them with present-day standards [then] we realize the extent of progress made by the Union in the effort to make life worth while for these workers'.[16] Union efforts continued to be well rewarded for a time after nationalization in 1948 because by then there was a serious shortage of workers.

One further area of improvement in this century came with the development of technology. Steam tugs and steam boats did much to reduce accidents and improve conditions in estuarial waters in the nineteenth century, but on canals such vessels were few. Internal-combustion engines suited this area better and were first used to propel canal boats in the early years of this century. Their use spread only slowly at first but they, in turn, did contribute to a great reduction in accidents. The boatmen and their families adapted themselves to the new technology with remarkable ease. Even as late as 1926 Llewellyn had known of no accidents involving their use. There was now no need for the crew to be forever jumping on and off the boats between locks, a fruitful cause of accidents. The engine was more easily accessible and obedient than a distant and sometimes rebellious horse. Gone was the task of trudging behind the animal, easing the work load of the whole crew as well as speeding up the business of boating. The ever-present dangers, all too frequently recorded—of injury from the swift unexpected kick of a fretful animal, from feet being trampled on, from startled creatures running amok—became a thing of the past for many boat people.

Internal-combustion engines also reduced danger from less visible sources. 'These boats', a Ministry of Health report concluded in 1934, 'are notable for improvement in design in ventilation and lighting, and also for the provision of sanitary conveniences, taking the form of chemical closets situated in the engine room.' On the narrow waterways the motor boat invariably towed a 'butty' boat which, by dividing a family between two cabins, further helped to reduce overcrowding on the waterways.

Motor boats were lit by electricity which, by replacing the uncertain oil lamp, again contributed to a reduction in accidents. The new technology did bring some fresh dangers however, as when a keel carrying 18,000 gallons of petrol blew up near Doncaster in 1929. The explosion was heard $3\frac{1}{2}$ miles away and shook the houses in the vicinity. The captain, J. Wilburn, was blown into the canal, but the mate who was driving the horse threw him a line and was able to get him out and to Doncaster Infirmary suffering from extreme burns and scalds.[17]

More tragic was a similar accident at Keadby on the Sheffield & South Yorkshire Canal.

The barge *Two Sisters* was filling up with benzoline. . . . The captain and his youthful mate aged 15 years were aboard attending to the filling of the tanks, when suddenly an explosion occurred which split the boat into two, instantly killing the captain and his mate. The captain's son aged 14 years, who had been ashore feeding the horse, was in the act of stepping on the barge when the explosion occurred. He was thrown to the ground but escaped injury. The shock to the lad when he saw what had happened to his father may be imagined.[18]

II

The Number One Kings

W. H. King was an unusual boatman. He could read and write—and in 1895 he kept a diary to prove it. King was no Greville or Pepys. From the first day of the year to the last, when he finally laid down his laboured pen, we read only of how he 'lay at Croxley', 'Emptyd the pair and came to Cassio Bridge', went from 'Cassio Bridge to fishery' and so on.[1]

King was the captain of a narrow boat and the vessel was either his own or hired. He was thus a 'bye-boatman' or 'bye-trader'—more popularly known in this century as a 'Number One'—and one of a rare breed, for only about 6 per cent of all boatmen worked their own boats in the 1890s. It had always been the ambition of almost every waterman to own his own craft. Many of Pickfords' boatmen, for instance, back in the Canal Age, had endured the endless, often wretched, toil of fly-boat working sustained by the dream that one day they would leave to trade on their own—and some of them did—but even then, in the heyday of the canals, owner boatmen were probably few.[2] It was also a constantly changing few. King's experiences explain why this might be so.

The name of King's boat eludes us. He always referred to it as 'ours'. 'Ours' always travelled in company with *The Four Brothers*, both pulled by one horse. The musty pages of a boat register at Paddington reveal that on 17 July 1887 the narrow boat *The Four Brothers* was registered in the name of Edward King. It turns out that Edward King was none other than the lad who had escaped—minus trousers—from the boat of his kidnapper back in 1842. He stayed with his parents for a while, but having learned the art of inland navigation he was tempted back on to the canal as a fly-boat hand. Over the years he grew into a man who, though rather small in stature, was 'not afraid of any thing or any man or any dog and could swim like a fish'. He married and moved into slow boats. His wife bore him four sons (hence the *Four Brothers*), but she died at a comparatively early age. Meanwhile Edward had been converted to religion and would never work his boats on a Sunday, but instead visited the other boats and preached the gospel to the boat people. It may have been this which caused him to be known to all the canallers as 'Grandad' King.

By 1879 he was working for a Southall miller, Alfred Robinson, as captain of both the *Jolly Miller* and the *Troy Mills*, two narrow boats carrying flour, bran and pollard from Norwood Mills to Paddington. He relinquished command of the miller's boats in August 1885. What he did for the next two years until he turned up with *The Four Brothers* is a mystery. But at last he was a bye-boatman. Canal trading saw something of a revival in the late 1880s and early 1890s and he did well. He came to own several narrow boats, working them with his sons, to whom he sold the craft as the boys, and he, grew older. Late in life he married again, a widow with daughters living near Tring. Around the turn of the century he retired and moved with them to Yorkshire, his wife's native county, where he died in 1907.

William Harry King, known always as Harry, was one of the 'four brothers', born in 1868 at Castle Street, Berkhamsted, but he lived most of his early life on the boats. In the very few months spent ashore he did manage to get some schooling, but the diarist was largely self-taught. He married the daughter of the lock-keeper at Watford Park locks in 1888 when he was twenty and the union produced nine children, six boys and three girls. He determined that they should have the education that he had missed and, as the older ones grew out of infancy, he rented a cottage at Apsley End for his wife and children. The chances are that Mrs King and the earlier children were with him in 'ours' in the year of the diary. Who was in *The Four Brothers* remains a mystery. Perhaps it was 'Grandad' King himself, now aged sixty-four. The only certainty is that 'ours' was captained by the twenty-seven year old Harry King.

That year of 1895 began inauspiciously, not only for the Kings but for all canal-boat people—demonstrating one of the difficulties felt by bye-boatmen in particular—for the water highways soon became paralysed through severe frost. On 7 January 'ours' and *The Four Brothers* 'lay at Ivinghoe on account of ice'. Not until the 9th were they released and the struggling horse and boatmen able to force a way—in the wake of the ice-boat no doubt—the thirteen miles or so to Fenny Stratford, but then they again 'lay at fenny lock froze up'. It was the 14th before the Kings were able to break out once more and head for Charity Colliery. The worst of the frost seemed to have passed as they loaded both boats with slack and confidently headed south. All went well. They made Croxley Mill (Harefield), unloaded and turned north again—but barely reached Berkhamsted, for on 30 January the ice closed in again and held the two boats 'froze up till 1st of March'. After these twenty-nine days of imprisonment they struggled desperately on to Ivinghoe, a mere 11 miles in two days, where they were again in the grip of the ice until the elements finally relented on the 6th. In the first sixty-five days of 1895 they had worked only twenty-four.

It seems unlikely that the Kings could have escaped the privation which was the lot of all canal-boat people during those hard weeks. On 13 February the chairman of the Grand Junction Company reported that 'owing to the canal being frozen great distress prevailed amongst the boatmen and their families at several

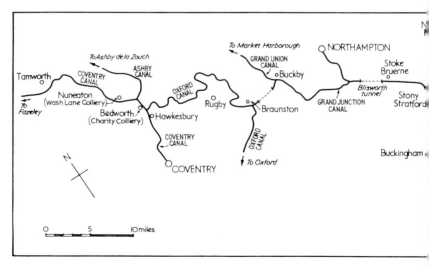

Canals where the Kings worked

points on the Canal and he had given instructions for temporary relief to be afforded in the shape of bread soup etc.' As compared with other outdoor workers laid off, they were at an added disadvantage for, as John Brydone pointed out, 'there was not only the masters of the boats, their wives and families to feed etc., but their horses had also to be cared for: the horse alone—for food and stabling—costing from 10s to 13s per week'.[3] As independents the Kings could not even draw advances against future earnings as company boatmen could, but had to dip into their financial reserves, if they had any. Whatever hardships they may have suffered we can only surmise, for on this the diary is silent. Still, the Kings were more fortunate than others as quite a few canals were frozen for seven or eight weeks. It is easy to understand how some boatmen, having just bought their boat perhaps, hoping for a good start to their trading venture in the difficult first months and years, found their hopes dashed and themselves back as company boatmen.

The Kings' troubles melted with the ice for, happily, weather conditions seem to have interfered little with their work for the remainder of the year. Only on 20 July and on one other day did they have to stop work and 'lay on account of wet day'. Conversely, on 6 August there was a shortage of water in the canal

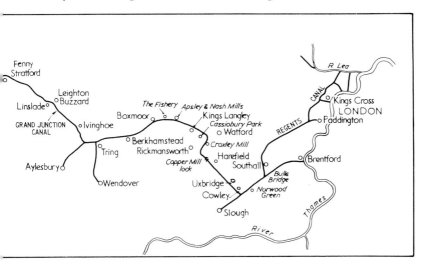

because at Marsworth they had to lighten 'our pair in two lighteners'. It was a short-lived problem. Three days later they were able to move 56 tons of cement from Shadbolt's (a forerunner of British Portland Cement), at Harefield, to Rugby. The largest tonnage ever carried by the two boats was 30 on 'ours' and $30\frac{1}{2}$ on *The Four Brothers* when they were working the deeper London end of the Grand Junction.

With the ice gone, periods of inactivity were rare. No doubt there was a backlog of cargoes to be transported after the freeze, for there were none of those long periods of waiting to load and unload and other delays which so bedevilled the lives and finances of the boatmen and were especially serious for the owner boatmen. The longest delay they had was two and a half empty days in April spent waiting to load sand at Sandhole Bridge, Linslade. Only fourteen full working days were lost in this way throughout the whole year, but coming on top of the freeze-up that was serious enough.

None the less the Kings' 'docking money' seems to have survived the frost, for, on 30 August, they came from 'fenny lock to thompsons dock high house and had our boat pulled out'. Repairs were carried out until 4 September when they 'Had our boat put in the water and pulled the 4 Bros out on the dock'. The other boat must have been in better condition for by the 6th they 'Had the 4 Bros. in the water and started with the pair'.

It was this docking business that saw the downfall of many an independent. Some were careless in putting money aside, preferring to spend it in the beer shop; others did not make enough to put money aside through no fault of their own; many drew on their reserves because of an 1895-type frost, a drought, a period of bad trade. They put off the regular docking hoping to get by—then the oakum fell out, the boat would sink, and the boatmen had to return to company boating.

If any boats needed regular docking it was those of the 'number ones'. Very few watermen could afford to buy a new vessel—a narrow boat fluctuated in price from around £60–100 for much of the Canal Age rising to around £150 by 1875 and to £300–400 by the 1920s and 1930s with barges being perhaps double those amounts. Flats and keels were even more expensive. During the years of the French Wars (1793–1815) inflation pushed up the price, with sails and rigging, to something approaching £1,000 and even in the 1820s and 1830s a fully rigged flat was still costing between £500 and 800. Unrigged flats were costing around £400 for most of the second half of the nineteenth century.

Some did manage to start off with a new boat. In the Midlands there were boat-building clubs. A group of boatmen formed themselves into a society, paid so much a week into the funds and when there was enough money the first boat was ordered from a local boat-builder, with whom a special price had been negotiated. The boat was finished, lots were drawn and the first lucky boatman was off to a good start. He had to keep up his subscriptions until every one had a boat and then the society was wound up.

Some boatmen made similar arrangements direct with a boat-builder, paying so much a week before and after the boat was built. But, for most, new boats were just too expensive to contemplate and they began with a second-hand vessel often in a rickety condition. Maybe they graduated on to a better one, more often they sank back into company boating.

Owning a flat was even more difficult and very few managed it. There were only four owner-masters in the Mersey coal/salt trade in 1795. The toll sheets of the Sankey Navigation show that there was probably little change over the years, for in January 1826 only one flat passing on that waterway was steered by its owner. This at a time when the waterways were supreme.

For some unknown reason there seem to have been more owner keelmen. According to Charles Hadfield, 'most of the Humber boatmen were independent'. Dr Taylor concluded that, 'Practically all the keels at this time [mid-nineteenth century] were owned by their captains . . .'. Harry Fletcher, himself a keel hand in the early years of this century, wrote, 'A keel cost about £450 and many captains bought their own by paying a deposit and working off the balance from their earnings. It took them fifteen to twenty years to clear the debt, depending on how well they managed to get cargoes'. There are few statistics available, however, to confirm the importance (which has perhaps swelled with time) of these independents. If only 6 per cent were 'working on their own account' over the country as a whole in the 1890s, the proportion of owner keelmen, at that time at least, could not have been all that significant.

Two of the 1795 flats give us some indication as to the types of vessels owned by flatmen. Thomas Haslehurst worked his 50-ton *Compleat* between Frodsham, Liverpool and the Sankey Navigation with his son, Joseph; and he had given his *Frodsham Trader* to another son, John. We get an inkling of the value of the family flats when Thomas died in 1798, for although he left property in Frodsham and elsewhere, and his flat *Compleat*, the total value of the estate still did not exceed £70; nor was the *Frodsham Trader* much of a gift to his son. His will mentioned 'whereas my said son John has had and received from me one vessel or flatt which he had caused to be condemned or pulled to pieces and value of this to be deducted from his share . . .'. A case of the foolhardy young son driving the family treasure on the rocks perhaps? More likely the *Frodsham Trader* was so rotten that John had to get rid of it before it sank beneath him.[4] Again, when John Hind died in 1816, although he left to his wife Elizabeth 'Household goods . . . money . . . my two Flats belonging to the Port of Liverpool' and other items, the total value of the estate did not exceed £200.[5] There were a lot of clapped-out vessels worked by 'bye-traders' on rivers and canals not only during the Canal Age, but down through to the end of canal carrying—although the Kings' boats probably did not fall into this category after 6 September 1895.

After the docking, to make up for lost time, they 'worked all the night and came to Wash Lane' a prodigious distance probably over forty miles. On several other occasions they laboured on into the next day. May 2, for example, found them at Slough where they 'Put half a thousand bricks [12,000 the previous day] on ours 13,000 + half on the 4 Bros and came in all night to Paddington tunnell'.

The speed with which they generally loaded and unloaded the boats confirms that the Kings were indeed a hard-working family. On one occasion in particular in two days they off-loaded about fifty tons of coal at the Copper Mill, moved a mile or so to Shadbolt's, loaded both boats with 14,000 bricks each and still made Cowley well down the canal before stopping for the night.

They worked long hours too. On the more distant runs between Wash Lane and Copper Mill they averaged about twenty-two miles a day winter and summer when loaded (excluding the starting and finishing days). At $1\frac{1}{2}$–2 mph their working day must often have exceeded twelve hours and in winter it must have entailed travelling part of the time during the hours of darkness. Empty they covered more ground, about thirty miles a day in summer and twenty-seven in winter.

The nearest they ever came to a holiday was on 25 and 26 December when they 'lay at coppermill' and another two days spent unaccountably at Paddington Stop. Perhaps they reckoned that they had holidayed enough in February—or that one rest day a week was enough, for as well as being hard working the Kings of the diary were conscious of the sanctity of the Sabbath. Unlike many others on the 'cut', not once did they stir on a Sunday. Perhaps the evangelical 'Grandad' King *was* aboard *The Four Brothers*? Not necessarily. Trevor King remembers that his grandfather Harry was as religious as his great-grandfather, never worked on Sunday and always attended chapel wherever the boats were moored. 'He must have been in every nonconformist chapel from Hertfordshire to Warwickshire. If there was no chapel in the area he would attend an Anglican service.'

Time has lent enchantment to the condition of the 'number one' as well as increased his number and importance. Many have warmed their hearts at the thought of these men, home at last from the years of Spartan life on the fly-boats, shaking off the discipline of company boating to drift off in the bosom of their family—happy, carefree and independent—wandering wherever there was a load. At their journey's end they would polish their gleaming brasses with pride as they waited to unload yet another fruitful cargo. Romantic and appealing though such ideas might be, they give a totally false picture of the type of life led by these people.

The first problem was to find a cargo. All the best value cargoes were carried by the big companies, as for that matter were many of the less valuable ones. The middle and even low value goods were creamed off by the hundreds of small carriers including manufacturers who owned boats merely to transport their own raw materials and finished goods—salt proprietors, iron-masters, glass-makers, and so on—all substantial concerns in spite of their relatively small fleets. Owner boatmen were usually restricted to the least valuable materials, the most unpleasant and the most awkward, because the low profit margins did not tempt the large companies.

The next problem was to get a regular cargo for it was no use having one boat load only to have to wait a month for the next. In addition all long-distance transport operators have had the problem of finding *back carriage*. Its availability to small operators like owner boatmen meant the difference between profit and loss. There was a sort of grapevine in the canal world. A note from the Cromford Iron Company in 1849 circulated the information, 'If you see any boatmen wanting to load kindly inform them that we want plenty of boats to load pig iron and oblige'.[6] But this was all rather haphazard.

The Kings were invariably successful in finding a return cargo. Even so, on thirty-seven full days in 1895 one or both boats travelled empty, although thirteen of these were associated with the dislocations caused by the frost and the docking of the boats. Cargoes for off loading along the long route to the Wash Lane colliery (it took about eleven working days for the round trip) were the hardest to come by, but they very often found something for a part of the way at least, usually cement and other building materials. These were picked up at Shadbolt's, conveniently near the Copper Mill at Harefield where the coal was unloaded. Alternatively, they would pick up cement, etc at Harefield and continue south to Paddington or Kings Cross, there to load up with breeze and ash to be used in the making of bricks at the brickfields on the Slough arm. In turn the bricks provided another load to be brought back to London. Wherever they unloaded, another cargo seemed to await them near by.

The trading pattern does suggest skilful organization on the part of the Kings, an essential quality for survival in what was often a precarious business—and not all owner boatmen were so skilful. Their skill was enhanced by knowledge of where and when loads were to be had and planning accordingly. This experience was acquired not by wandering all over the countryside, but by restricting themselves generally to the main line of canal between London–Brentford and Wash Lane, and the Slough arm. They worked for the same, if numerous, customers, and they carried the same cargoes; less valuable goods like bricks, coal, cement, breeze, ash, gravel and, if they were lucky, timber.

Plates 31, 32 *and* 33 The Kings: Edward 'Grandad' King (*above left*) (*M. E. Ware*); W. H. 'Harry' King with his wife in retirement (*above right*) (*Trevor King*); their sons aboard *Forget-me-not c* 1914 (*below*), David (*left of the chimney*) was killed in France shortly after this photograph was taken (*Trevor King*)

Table 2

365	Days
52	Sundays
—	
313	Working days
31	Full working days frozen up
—	
282	
14	Full working days waiting to load, unload, or waiting a cargo★
—	
268	
10	Other waiting working? days: 25–26 December, 6 docking, 2 (unaccountable) at Paddington Stop
—	
258	
37	Full days travelling empty one or both boats★
—	
221	Total days fully and gainfully employed

★ Some *parts* of days spent in this way not included.

One suspects that the Kings were typical 'bye-boatmen', and that others, too, limited themselves to a definite area, although there were some, according to Frederick Morton, who would 'go anywhere'. He also pointed to another function of the owner boatmen. Certain carriers, like Fellows Morton & Clayton, brought back more from the ports than they took and they then used small carriers, and especially number ones, to bring back the surplus. 'If a man takes a load from the Stourbridge district to London,' he explained in 1906,

> . . . a load of firebricks . . . we very frequently load that man's boat back for him. . . . We do a great deal of that sort of thing . . . [and] we do not interfere with them because we get practically— although they may take a little traffic from us in one direction— the advantage is we have more loading back again from the ports . . . so that we are very glad to avail ourselves of their boats.[7]

Sometimes number ones were actually hired by the large carriers for quite long periods of time, for another of their functions was that they acted as a reserve supply of boats to be drawn on by the canal industry in times of brisk trade, as in 1874 when the Bridgewater Company had more potters' material to move than they could handle and they hired some bye-boatmen from the Black Country. On the Mersey too, in 'thronged' times, owner flatmen, few though they were, would often be hired by the larger companies. In good times number ones moved up the canal scale to carry higher value goods than they normally would—in bad times they slipped down again and some slipped out—the improvident, the inefficient, the unlucky.

The nearest thing to security for the owner boatman was a regular long-term contract. Thus did Harry King prosper. Trevor King has filled in the missing years after the diary ended so exactly, but so intriguingly, on 31 December 1895. In 1898 Harry bought the wide boat *Chesham* brand new and worked her in bringing regular cargoes of wheat from Brentford to T. W. Toovey's at Kings Langley, returning with cement from Shadbolt's Harefield cement works. Alas, trade slackened again and in 1907 he was forced to sell the *Chesham* to Shadbolt's and return to company boating as captain of a pair of horse boats for Emmanuel Smith, Canal Carriers, working the London–Midland traffic. In 1908 he once again went independent with two narrow boats purchased from W. E. Costins of Castle Dock, Berkhamsted. After a year or so of freelance work he was lucky in getting a contract for the coveted 'Mill Job'. He became one of about fourteen number ones bringing coal on a regular basis from the Warwickshire coal field to John Dickinson's Apsley, Nash and Home Park mills in Hertfordshire doing an average of twenty-five trips a year. He continued with this trade until 1923 when hard times again forced him to sell his boats.

Some boatmen were cagey and kept a foot in both camps. While continuing to work for a carrier with one boat, they took their own along and had the best of both worlds. There was a similar type of caginess among the flatmen. The ownership of some flats was a very complex business. The *Mary*, for example, a coal/salt flat based on Winsford was owned in 1795 by three Liverpool merchants, a Cheshire merchant and James Magee, a small salt-pit proprietor. They owned other flats on the same principle. It was probably a way of splitting the risks and the capital burden throughout the trade. A few flatmen were involved in this joint ownership.

The Mersey flatmen, however, were not men to put all their eggs in one basket. Richard Buckley owned a fifth share in the *Fox* in 1795, but Samuel Weedall was the master. Buckley himself was the captain of one of the flats of a Leftwich salt proprietor—Thomas Bridge.[8] There were others like him. Part sharing of a flat was an old established principle. John Ashton, flatman, of Northwich, died in 1773 and wished to 'give and bequeath unto my said wife all my fourth part or share of the Betty flatt John Hallaway master, with the rigging and Tarkle thereto belonging which was purchased from James Walton and partner'.[9]

In this way a few flatmen came to own a whole vessel in time. Robert Denton, who had been the master of Robert Poole's *Nancy* in 1795, owned a half share in the *Swarrow* with Poole at the time of the latter's death in 1809. By the time of Denton's death in 1836 the whole flat was his.[10]

The same practice of share holding was common in Yorkshire too. In 1843 there was sold at Masborough near Rotherham a '$\frac{1}{4}$ SHARE of the BILLY BOY, called the "MONICA" of which John Rhodes of Thorne is the Captain and Proprietor of the remaining shares'.[11]

Owner boatmen did have a role to play in the canal world—so long as they knew their place, for not all carriers, especially the canal company carriers, were as obliging and tolerant as Frederick Morton. They took steps to squeeze out the bye-boatmen if they became too numerous or encroached on trade that was not considered to be rightfully theirs. Still, they had a small place and they fulfilled a variety of useful functions. On some canals conditions were particularly favourable to owner boatmen. On the Worcester & Birmingham, the Oxford and, to a lesser extent, on the Grand Junction and in keel country there was less interference from the large companies, or there were remunerative trades especially suited to them. In such areas, and in others too, when there was a period of continuous prosperity the vessels of the number ones often gave evidence of the pride these people took in their craft. It was the same in the USA where, though they were equally few in number, the 'immaculate, neatly painted cabins of some of the independent boatmen, with attractive curtains at the windows, spotless linen on the bunks, good lamps, and stationary wash-stands . . .' stood out from the company boats.[12] But times were often hard for the number ones. They would struggle on in leaky, often overcrowded craft, the peeling paintwork of their cabins serving as a faint memory of better years, rather than give up their freedom and independence until a frost, a collision or the death of a horse forced the inevitable upon them.

There were a few success stories. Captains took up bye-boating at the right time and grew into fully-fledged carriers. Samuel Parkes, from being a hard-working boatman, built up a successful coal business in Birmingham, owning nine boats by 1839.[13] Albert Wood, a boatman for William Jackson, in 1894 bought out the Sowerby Bridge business and expanded it to forty-five boats before he was forced to give up in 1937.[14] John Griffith, a Bed-worth canal carrier, came up through the mill with his father. There were fourteen of them altogether, all except four born in their father's boat.

'May I ask how you got your present position?' enquired a curious committee man.

'My father started he bought a boat himself; then he got from one to two and three, and then he started carrying. Then he managed for Fellows Morton & Clayton. He managed for them for five years. That gave me a chance to get education.'[15]

And there is the apocryphal story of Samuel Barlow, 'Big Sam', a 'joey' boatman in the Birmingham area who was always drunk. His wife died and he found considerable savings hidden beneath her bed in their boat. Stricken with remorse he stopped drinking and worked with increasing fury to create a large coal carrying company of close on a hundred boats by the late 1930s—the Samuel Barlow Coal Co Ltd—not to be confused with 'Little Sammy' Barlow of Tamworth whose boats were taken over by the 'Limited' in 1957.

There were others, but the role of boatmen and ex-boatmen as owners of boats throughout the whole of the canal carrying period was probably extremely limited.

The greatest proportions came, paradoxically, towards the end of commercial carrying in the 1920s and 1930s—bleak times. This was because two of the factors which had kept the proportions of bye-boatmen low for so long were less applicable. Many of the big carrying companies ceased trading in the 1920s because it was no longer profitable, but some of the goods were still there to be carried. Owner boatmen had always had an uneasy existence in the presence of the big carrying companies (especially in the north west and north-west Midlands) which used them or froze them out according to their whim or the state of the trade. With this restraint much reduced in the 1920s, and after the relatively prosperous years of the war and post-war boom, many enterprising boatmen got themselves a boat and went trading—enterprising or desperate, for many of the boatmen were those thrown out of work by the big companies. There were plenty of second-hand boats about—cheap to buy or hire—because of the surplus capacity. This gave some men their chance.

It was a slim chance, however, for many of the 11 per cent working on their own account in 1921 were forced to give up. There were only 9 per cent by 1931 according to the Census returns. Others were probably hanging on desperately for it was not so easy as it had been to return to company boating. Of the waterway labour force 13 per cent was 'out of work' and many more were under-worked.

Owner boatmen continued to dwindle in number, but then so did the numbers of all watermen. Now they have all gone from the waterways.

12
A Distinct Being

Sinners, alas, are often more interesting than saints and we have dwelled upon the disreputable elements; the unpleasant aspects of canal life. It is only fair that we should, since so often these matters have been glossed over in romantic nostalgia. Time has lent enchantment to a lost people, whereas the reality was somewhat different. It is only since the boat people have gone that their image has improved.

Many people, at almost any time that the waterways were carrying goods, would have agreed with the *Standard* reporter when he concluded in 1877 'Canal boatmen are, speaking generally, not the pleasantest fellows to have to do with . . .' because that was the popular image of the canal folk—or those on boats at least.

There is no denying that it is more pleasant to read about some canal people than it would have been to meet them. For all that, there were many good things about canal life and folk, and those aspects will hardly be gleaned from the annual reports of the NSPCC, from the utterings of ardent reformers and zealous vicars, or from the crime columns of newspapers.

Though there was much that was hard and unsavoury about women and children living on board, there was something rather special about the family boat at its best. The strange blend of domesticity and nomadism, always travelling from one place to another, never entirely certain of the next destination and this, in a small cabin, involved organization and the co-operation of the whole family. In such a small space it meant that everything had its place and had to be in it, which explains why boat people for the most part kept their vessels tidy and clean. For the women in particular it meant planning ahead for the washing; the preparation in advance of meals that could be eaten quickly and easily 'on the go'; the buying in of provisions for an uncertain period perhaps in the few minutes that the boat took to pass a lock.

'You just have to know how long food will last and plan accordingly,' explained Rose Whitelock, one of the last of the narrow-boat women.[1]

They were an organized people. During the Great War a group of men found themselves in a hut with much to do under trying conditions.

'There was one man in the hut who considered it, quite unconsciously, his duty to look after everyone else,' another inmate remembered.

In a quiet unassuming way this man, Collinson, would do what needed doing, bringing much help and comfort to the others.

'Collinson,' he added, 'was a British bargee.'[2]

Each member of a boat family from an early age felt a strong sense of responsibility to the others, the boat and the work.

'We all work together in this family,' explained Jack Skinner another boater who stayed on the 'cut' almost to the end, 'We've got no special jobs. When any one of us—that's kids too—see a job wants doing, we do it that's all.'

There was a family togetherness that has now virtually disappeared from our society.

That unity might often have seemed to be based more upon necessity than love. Mr Clarke was surprised and touched to see a boatman and his child playing a game of kissing as he steered the boat.

'What a happy thing it would be for both parents and children,' he wrote, 'if there were more love and tenderness and more care for the little Johns and Marys on the water.'[3]

Still, though the boat parents were often unthinking in the way they put their children to work; casual in the matter of their education; ignorant in modern ways of rearing them; demanding (harshly by modern standards), and getting, respect and obedience, they were not as heartless as some seemed to think. If the difficulties and trials of their lot made them seem hard, dour and sometimes uncouth, there was much of the Israeli 'sabra' about them—a hard and sometimes prickly exterior masked a surprising tenderness within.

John Brydone knew the boat people almost as well as they knew themselves. Although never afraid to castigate them for their short-comings he was concerned that the public saw parents in an unfair and unfriendly light. He gave a moving description of a near tragic incident at a lock in 1889. A boatman's eight year old son was romping excitedly and happily around the lock.

'. . . suddenly the mother, having missed him from her sight uttered one of the most piercing and heart-rending screams I have ever heard and then shouted. "Where is the lad? He's drowned!" '

Sure enough the youngster had fallen into the lock—but with some effort he was, fortunately, rescued.

'I shall never forget', the inspector wrote, 'the look of intense agony, fear and thankfulness which were alternatively and rapidly depicted upon that anxious mother's face. So long as the danger and uncertainty existed she seemed endowed with super-human energy and presence of mind, but when all danger was passed she returned to the cabin and sank down speechless and seemed almost paralysed.' The father too expressed his concern in a different, but equally moving way.[4]

Parents became increasingly conscious of the disadvantages that their children suffered.

'When you're working the boats you can't look after the kids properly or give them regular meals,' Violet Ward explained. 'You're worried about them falling in too. And I want mine to be able to read and write.'[5]

In fact many boaters left the 'cut' exactly because of their children. Even in the emotionally charged debates of the 1920s the NSPCC admitted that there was less wilful cruelty on the boats than among shore dwellers.

The relationship between a waterman and his wife could again hardly be described as tender on the face of it. Mr Clark on another towpath walk near Dudley Port fell into conversation with a toll-collector.

'I saw something the other day, I never saw on the canal among boat people in my life before,' remarked the collector.

He went on to explain how he had seen a boat woman leaving the boat to go to her home in the village nearby. The parting with her husband took the tollman quite by surprise—'the boatman took hold of his wife's hand, gave it a loving shake, and after speaking a kindly word, leaned forward and *kissed her cheek*'.

"John, mind and take care of yourself," she called out tenderly and affectionately, as the boat moved away.

"All right," John smiled back.

'Never in all my life before,' repeated the toll-collector, 'had I seen a boatman on the canal kiss his wife, or boat couple part . . . with such expressions of tender and loving regard for each other's welfare and safety.'[6]

Still, even if 'the cross look, and the gruff and cold "good morning"' that he had more commonly heard (if he had heard any words at all) suggested that relationships between man and wife were generally sterner on the canal, it is a fact that boat couples were remarkably faithful to each other. In three years Sister Hanson knew only one case of a couple parting and they came together again soon afterwards. She did have a wife turning up one morning with two black eyes. 'But they were not true boating people and didn't stay long.' Boaters seemed to suffer none of the emotional problems which bedevilled and still bedevil others in society.[7] Forrester Clayton of Thomas Clayton (Oldbury) Ltd, attributed this to the fact that the husband and family were always together. In twenty-five years his firm had only had two boat couples 'going wrong'.[8] Llewellyn remarked in 1919 that 'the ordinary run of boatmen and their wives are of a very moral disposition and dislike, or at any rate have no fancy for, many things that attract the ordinary shore-going classes'. Everything was open and above board.

'Well, Master,' explained one boatman, 'we ain't got no back doors here!'

Still, appearances were all important and Selina Dix, the Coventry head mistress, judged things very much by appearances in 1920. 'Well I have visited the boats . . . and I think anyone who has visited the boats and examined the sleeping places would think it inconceivable that there should be a high standard of morality . . .'.

The inconceivable was none the less conceivable since it was widely acknowledged, among those who knew the boaters, that illegitimacy was very rare. Tim Wilkinson pointed out that through being so close to their parents boat children discovered about natural things in a natural way, but there were very real taboos. John Redknap, his young hand, explained why he would not have sexual relations with any boating girl before marriage. 'Because I'd get killed and so would she. My dad and her dad would knock all shapes of hell out of me, and she'd cop it right and proper from her mum and dad.'[9]

The control of sexual passion (or lack of it) has always caused problems in civilized societies though attitudes vary from one society to another, and from time to time. The boat people in fact seem to have come to terms with the problems in a satisfactory way at a time when many in nineteenth- and twentieth-century society found sex an uneasy bed fellow. Certainly the 'morality' of the boat people within their own community compared very favourably with land people by the standards of the time, as a general rule, and the chances are that they always had done, even though there was no shortage of young boatmen as eager as any others to sow their wild oats—off the 'cut'.

The dishonesty of the waterway folk was exaggerated too. Some of them stole from the canal banks, cheated with tolls, pilfered from cargoes (although in the case of coal this came to be widely recognized as a perk). Many of them did none of these things. Richard Heath, a Stourport carrier, reckoned that by 1841 'the Men themselves are very much improved; we have a great many Men who are sober, honest and well-conducted', and other carriers said much the same.[10] The Mersey and Weaver flatmen were considered to be a particularly elevated class by those who were in a position to know (in contrast to the views of some vicars). On the point of pilfering, though it was definitely on the increase during the French Wars and in the bad years immediately after, there was still more honesty than dishonesty. 'We have not been under the necessity of prosecuting any of the servants upon the navigation for pilfering during the period of ten years and a half; no instance of it', Thomas Lingard, superintendent of the Old Quay, insisted in 1825.[11] In 1817 David Marling, a buyer of salt, explained that he 'dealt with respectable owners of flats who employ servants they can put the greatest confidence in'. Thomas Barker did not think his firm had 'lost a bushel of salt in forty years' and other salt proprietors agreed with him.[12] Pennington admitted 'there were some good men who ran Hargreaves' fly boats for ten, twenty and thirty years and who might have been entrusted with untold gold'.

The watermen often took the blame for 'depredations' that they had not themselves been involved in. Canal boats carried items of considerable value during the Canal Age and there were plenty of shady characters waiting for an opportunity to make off with them. In Cheshire there was the Rud Heath Gang operating in 1817. Another gang was responsible for a large number of thefts from boats and the wharf at Banbury. In 1798 William Rials, a butcher, was found guilty of stealing clothing from a box on board John Tootle's vessel moored at Doncaster.

Among themselves and the people with whom they came into close contact there was a strict code of honesty that the waterway folk generally adhered to. They might try to 'do' one another on a deal, but once settled the money would be paid in full. A loan to a boatman was as safe as a treasury bill. One NSPCC inspector recalled how he relieved a family going through hard times 'to the extent of 5s two years ago; the man repaid the money with thanks, last month'.

Hollins explained how in the 1840s and 1850s he frequently found

> . . . no Bible in the cabin and no money in the men's possession to purchase one; and time after time have I left Bibles and testaments behind Me, on the understanding that the men were to pay for them when they returned to Gloucester. These payments were made in all parts of the city. . . .

Advances or other loans from employers (such as to buy a horse) were invariably repaid to the nearest penny.

Proudly independent in spirit they refused to 'sponge' on anybody. Only in times of severe frost or other hardship would they reluctantly approach people like missionaries to ask for financial help.

There was, too, much that was interesting and beautiful about the life. Some argued that the waterway folk were resistant to its charms.

> Stolid and illiterate, they saw nothing beautiful in the scenery through which some of their journeys were made. Stretches of undulating country backed by wooded heights or pleasant fields and glens, decked with flowers that lined the waterway, had not as

a rule, half the charm for them that the smoke rising from the chimney of a village public-house had. . . . [13]

Such a view would be wrong. Many boat people did appreciate the life though they might on occasion curse their lot. Paddy North, in the 1920s, put into words the feelings of many boat people.

If there is anything I dislike, it is noise—like travelling on the railway with its rattle, smoke and bustle! To come back afterwards to the barge and hear the gentle clatter of Gypsy on the towpath as he plays tunes on his tin nose-box, is like walking in the sunshine (from a bad dream) with the morning dew on your face. And to hear the water swish at the bow of the *Gerda* as she goes along and smell the wind off the heather. . . . [14]

'It's a grand life,' said George Beechey contentedly in 1959, 'and there couldn't be a nicer way of travelling between London and Birmingham. It's a lot better and safer than that there M1 I'll be bound.' [15]

The advantages outweighed the disadvantages for Alf Best.

'It's a tough life in the winter, though it's not so bad when you are bred and born to it. It's a good life, too, with plenty of fresh air. You don't have to clock in and out and time is more or less your own.' [16]

The same kind of contentment could be found among many of the land workers. One group who cruised over some of the (more difficult) Midland canals in the 1950s paid testimony to the 'willing and cheerful help of the canal lengthsmen and lock-keepers. It is extraordinarily pleasant these days to find men who really like their jobs: they work long hours in all weathers to keep the waterways in sound condition'. [17]

Then there was the camaraderie of an evening captured so well by Rolt in his *Narrow Boat*, writing of the pleasant evening he spent with the boat people at the Bull and Butcher at Napton. An evening in the pub was virtually the only diversion open to the boatmen until radio and the cinema came along in this century. In the nineteenth century it was a common thing for them to finish their chores and drift into the pub where each fresh arrival would be 'hailed with uproarious welcome'.

By-and-by a 'harmony' . . . is originated, and a jolly red-faced man, with one hand in his pocket and the other holding his pipe, which anon will serve as a baton to conduct the chorus, breaks forth into a song with rarely less than eight verses, each verse being followed by a noisy and thirst creating chorus, in which all the company join. This will be followed . . . by a 'breakdown' or a 'step dance' in which the bargees, big and burly men that most of them are, excel, and the accompaniment will probably be played on a concertaina by one of the 'chaps' or on a wheezy violin....[18]

In the USA it was the same. At the locks and horse stations there were taverns and there would gather the crews of the boats which lay overnight in the vicinity 'and the squawk of the fiddle and wail of the accor-deen would mingle on the evening air with the rasp of rugged voices raised in song'.[19]

The bargemen would later, according to one prejudiced writer, turn out 'reeling into the open to quarrel or fight with any one with whom he may have differed, or, worse still, to continue his orgies in the cabin of his boat beside his wife and children'.[20]

Certainly there were such incidents, as there were on land too—diminishing as the century wore on—but boatmen were not at such roisterous proceedings every night, which rather grew spontaneously when a large number of boats chanced to tie up at one place. Even so they were 'off very early again in the morning; they do not let it interfere with their work'. Most of the American boatmen also 'carried their liquor remarkably well'.

Many in fact drank little, content with an occasional night in the pub. Very often the woman would spend her evening knitting, her husband taking a contemplative pipe, feet dangling from the cabin roof. Or they would chat with other boat people on the towpath or in the cabin.

Such gatherings were clearing houses for news. Boaters going away in different directions would carry it far and wide. At other times outpourings of information and instructions would be exchanged as the boats passed.

One and all they know each other's journeys . . . they will hail each other in passing while the two lines swing across.

'Good morning, Joseph!'

'Good morning, Harry!'

'If 'ee see Sam in Oxford tell 'en I've got that thare horse for 'en

196

whenever he wants to see 'er.'

And then no doubt may follow little scraps of canal gossip in voices rising as the distance increases between them. For never do they loiter. Time is a precious matter with them, and with them also necessity is their chronometer.[21]

There must be 'no stoppin' the boat'. 'It puts no bread on the loaf stoppin' here,' one boat woman admonished a missionary who was trying to tempt her to church.

Families became widely dispersed as the lads grew old enough to work a boat of their own and the girls married into another boat. It often happened that members of the family disappeared for years, though everyone knew where they were and how they were doing—if they stayed on the 'cut'. Aubertin described the passing of another couple of boats.

'How d'ye do, Jim?'

'How d'ye do, Harry?'

'Where for?'

'Macclesfield with bricks. What's your game?'

'Pleasure trip.'

'That was my brother,' the boatman explained to Aubertin. 'Haven't seen him a many a year.'[22]

They could be direct, especially the Yorkshire keelmen. The Reverend R. Clarke, recognized that they were 'blunt and out-

Plate 34 Keels and keel people at Warehouse Hill Wharf, Leeds, *c* 1914 (*Leeds Library*)

spoken; to a sensitive spirit they are rough indeed'. But he went on 'once you get to know them there are no finer people to mission among'.

If, on the face of it, they were rough, there was no denying they were tough. 'They are so hardy,' Sister Hanson remarked of the London and Birmingham boatmen, 'that they habitually leave the surgery door open in winter because they cannot stand the heat.' The grit of the keelmen was legendary. Joseph Eastwood was trimming the lamp in the cabin when some oil fell on his hand and clothing and in a moment he was on fire. The fire was quickly extinguished, but he was a mass of burns. The *Waterman* proudly recorded in July 1928 'let this tribute be paid to the grit and courage of Yorkshire boatmen—after the flames had been extinguished, while he must have been suffering almost incredible pain, Captain Eastwood *walked* from his keel to the Infirmary'. Though he lingered many weeks in hospital the captain eventually recovered completely.

This story of Yorkshire courage must be complemented with one of Lancashire heroism. Sadly the ending was more tragic.

The coal boat *Burnley*, owned by Bowaters of Hulme was proceeding through Sale towards Altrincham, when a boy named Edwin Holt (12) of Barnes's Yard, Bell Lane, Bury, who was at the helm, fell into the water. His aunt Mrs Sarah Ann Lee, a widow, who was lying ill in the bottom of the boat, heard the splash and saw the boy in the water. She attracted the attention of George Olive (39), of Knobb Inn, Little Lever, Bolton, the skipper, who at the moment was on the bank leading the horse. . . . Olive dived to the rescue and succeeded in reaching the boy, but suddenly he shouted 'Save the boy; never mind me,' let go of Holt, sank and was drowned [as was the boy]. . . . An additional sad circumstance is that the man Olive and Mrs Lee, whose late husband was killed during the War, were about to be married. A younger brother of the boy Holt was drowned at Castlefield, near Manchester, last October.[23]

Mr Clarke mentioned that all boat folk were 'a brave, sturdy people, patient and persevering to the core with a good heart beating beneath it all'.

The toughness of the keelmen was matched by their dour,

mischievous sense of humour. A Leeds man asked a keelman if he would favour him with a trip on the canal, and if so he would cheerfully work his passage.

'Certainly,' responded the keelman, 'Lead the horse.'

Cut off in many ways from the rest of society their ways were engagingly different. They conversed in a broad dialect which was impossible to localize. 'A bargee's accent seems to be coloured by every county he passes through,' said Jack Smethurst, an actor struggling to master it for a television play. Their language often consisted of mutilations of English such as when a boatman told the Reverend Davies in 1838, 'Sir, I think this working on the Sabbath will be "disbolished" '. Captain Randle spoke of 'useful' matches meaning lucifers. A 'scholar' or 'scollard' was someone who could read and write. Locks with guillotine-type doors and aqueducts became 'gullertynes' and 'ackerducks'.

There was an almost poetic onomatopaeic exactness about the use of some unorthodox words as when John Arnold heard a 'slump' or 'splunge' when something had been dropped into the canal. A beautiful blue 'bursticle' of flame was how a fly-boat man had described the preliminary explosion of benzoline on the *Tilbury* which was to spark off the Regent's Canal catastrophe. They had been 'warned from' fire when transporting explosives and though there was only a 'mere' fire in the cabin stove it had proved sufficient to start the explosion. Captain Randle could turn a particularly fine phrase. Though still hail and hearty he did admit 'I'm goin' a little at the bottom of my feet'.

Places were given unusual labels. Boats worked between 'Lunnon' and 'Brummagem' or 'Birningham'; passed through 'Maffers' [Marsworth], the 'Ganzees' [Walsall] and 'Tarbic' [Tardebigge]; took coal to the 'Leicester Light' [Leicester Power Station]. The bridge rebuilt after the 1874 explosion was known as 'Blow-up Bridge'. 'Soakem' was the keelman's name for Alexandra Dock, Hull, because the entrance was so rough. Hawkesbury Junction was 'Sutton Stop' to the boat people long after the Suttons had ceased to be toll-collectors there.

Intruders were instantly recognized as outsiders because they did not know the language. Boating was a very exclusive business. Those who were not born to it were never completely accepted by those who were.

Canal work involved such unnautical pursuits as 'shoving off' for casting off. A boat did not 'dock' but 'tied up', except when a man was told to 'take his boat to the dock' in which case he was sacked. His 'starting money' was to pay for the expenses of the trip. He lived in his 'cuddy'; put cargo in the 'stowage' and 'clawed up' the boat (put the tarpaulin on) which when loaded and deep in the water made the narrow boats look like 'attenuated hippopotomi floating down the African rivers'. He might be caught 'doing Wiggerham' (cheating the gauging system).

Many a waterman was known by his 'bye-name' rather than by his real name. There must be some profound psychological reason why there were so many nicknames on the waterways, but what that reason was remains obscure. It did add another colourful dimension to boating life not only in Britain but in Europe and America. There was Grandad King of course and Civil John, who was another devout Christian, working on the Shropshire Union. Other quirks of character and appearance were represented by Moody Sam, Big Sam, Little Sammy (Barlow), and Ratty. Harry Fletcher was always known as the White-Haired Kaffir. Nudger was a keelman who steered too close to other keels. Makeapenny was always looking for ways to make money. William Westwood was known as Powerful. Chocolate Charlie Atkins boated for Cadbury's for a part of his career and the name sticks with him still. At one time it was thought (incorrectly) that Birmingham Joe had been killed in the Regent's Canal explosion and there were others who carried their origins always with them like Banbury Bess, Eynsham Harry, and Stour. Jack Smith became known as General Shackleton because for many years he worked with a boatman nicknamed—General Shackleton. When General Shackleton I died, the mantle passed to him.

The origin of other bye-names is even more obscure if indeed those who bore them knew themselves. Harry Fletcher's father was always known, even in old age, as Young Jim, and his grandfather as Lemon Bill. Arthur Meredith answered to Arthur Ready, and there was Ikey Mo, Half Paddle Tommy, Moucher, Redman, St Peter and many others.

In almost every aspect of life the boat people seemed determined to put their distinctive stamp upon things as if the mundane matters of the everyday world demanded embellishment. Nowhere else but on the waterways could there be seen on the darkest dullest December day the *Rose in June* blooming upon the water. Eastern and oriental vistas might glide through London and Birmingham in the shape of the *Danube* and the *Indus* followed by the less romantic *Mersey* or *Irwell*. A suggestion of sea air might follow with the *Neptune* and the *Sea Flower*. Some boats hinted at the unity of family life—the *Henry and Alice*; *Mark and Louise*, *Four Brothers* and the *United Sisters*. The character of the boat people emerged from the *Perseverance*, *Industry*, *Defiance*, *Invincible*, *Envy None* and *Live and Let Live*. A word of caution was spread with the *Fools Rush In* or *Fools Will Be A Meddling*, and advice with *Never too late to mend*.

Harry King's wide boat was called *Chesham* because that was the birth place of his wife. His wife's favourite flower bloomed on the narrow boat *Forget-me-not*. Some boatmen liked to change the name of their boat whenever she was docked and re-painted. The *Forget-me-not* was renamed three times, becoming the *Orion*, *David* and *Euston*. David King, Harry's son, was killed in World War I.

Of course many boats were in the hands of large concerns, distinguished only by an impersonal number or letter, but the big companies usually had a system; trees one year, flowers the next, then birds, rivers and so on. 'Little Sammy' Barlow's boats were named after admirals; Shadbolt's after animals. One company had a run of countries, but three of them, *Germany*, *Austria* and *Turkey*, had to be re-registered under new names in 1914 as the steerers refused to work them.

As in almost all walks of life there were many different types of people on the waterways—rich and poor, good and bad, dirty and clean. One thing they all had in common was that they were nomads. Wanderers have always excited the enmity of settled populations. A man 'of no fixed abode' is often seen as a rogue. Men who have no homes and roots or who by the nature of their calling are often far from them, are men to be watched. Tramps, soldiers, sailors, lorry drivers are tolerated uneasily. People who have made a whole life-style of wandering, by necessity or desire, have carried more than their fair share of the burden of society's prejudices. Jews and Gypsies have proved useful scapegoats for centuries.

It is perhaps no coincidence that, as the uneven weight of suffering did begin to lift somewhat from the shoulders of these two unfortunate burdened races in early nineteenth-century Britain (if not in the world at large), there emerged a third group worthy of castigation. Here was a new pagan race of predators who, wherever they passed, supposedly left a trail of depredation and violence. Their mode of life became synonymous in the public mind with ignorance and squalor; drunkenness and sin.

There is no doubt that there were, and remained, some original characters on the waterways—and some whose originality came in the form of villainy. Aubertin would have disagreed. He voyaged on the waterways before World War I. 'I have met hundreds of bargees; among them were many rough diamonds, but not one ruffian.' He did concede that 'the rich man's game and even the poor man's chicken sometimes find their way into his cooking pot', and no doubt his view of ruffianism would have changed somewhat if it had been his chicken. Some regions had more than their fair share of such villains and of the worst aspects of canal-boat life—the north-west Midlands was one. There were definite groupings on the waterways. The Lancashire bargemen and flat-men did not mix much with the keelmen and all three considered themselves a cut above the narrow-boat people. In turn the narrow-boat men who worked to the south of Birmingham considered themselves to be superior to say the Black Country boatmen, and the Grand Junction people did not mingle too happily with the wide-boat men working the southern end of that canal and the Regent's Canal. 'Day' boat men, who worked their boats during the day and then went to their homes in Birmingham or Manchester each night, formed another somewhat separate group.

The *Standard* reporter did finally conclude that, though there were indeed some bad people on the waterways, many of the statements made about them were 'altogether overdrawn'. They were 'not so bad as they have been painted'. The finest testimony came from Owen Llewellyn who, in describing all the waterway people in 1930, after thirty-two years as chief inspector of canal boats, wrote how, in 1899,

> . . . as now I was able to report that, opportunities for education apart, there was very little amiss with the boat people. . . . I am . . . sad to leave . . . folk from whom in all my time I can honestly say

I have never had one cross word, let alone the type of language that ignorant humorists think it witty to attribute to them. 'Bargees' are decent folk in the best sense of the word, and the fact that they take very little interest in what other folk do and say and are content to get on with their work, is a clear proof of it. The debates and the correspondence aroused on the occasion of the late Canal Boats Bill showed that no class of worker stood in less need of supervision and their morals and morality were held up in public approval.[24]

13
Where Did They All Go?

'While it was economic to transport our coal in boats we did so,' said David Campbell, manager of the Braunston-based Samuel Barlow Coal Co Ltd in 1961, 'but the diesel road engine now does it more economically.' He added,

> We supply coal to the canal-side paper mills and other works in Hertfordshire and Middlesex. A pair of boats that run from the Warwickshire coalfield can load only once a week, with 50 tons between them. A lorry does the return journey in eight hours, five days a week, carrying 12 tons and in a week that's 20 per cent up on the boats.[1]

A lorry needs one driver; a pair of boats needed two, and ideally three, to work them. A road vehicle can also go from door to door, but, unless a factory is on the canal bank, a boat cannot. Costly transhipment is necessary.

Though he roused Leslie Morton's ire by saying it publicly, David Campbell put in a nutshell the cause of the demise of canal carrying in this century—the motor lorry. Since 1961 motorways and ever larger vehicles (and pipelines) have effectively killed off carrying on the wide waterways too.

Of course there were many things wrong with the canals—their bad state; the antiquated system of tolls; loading and unloading facilities that belonged to an earlier century; as well as the eighteenth-century mentality which still pervaded the minds of many in the canal world—but, from 1921, it was the increasing influence of the motor lorry which eroded canal transport.

By the end of World War II carrying on the narrow waterways was really finished as a sensible means of conveyance. None breathed a louder sigh of relief than the management and shareholders of the largest carrier—Fellows, Morton & Clayton—when nationalization put them out of business in 1948. State ownership kept carrying going for a little longer, as did the efforts of men who had always been involved in carrying, who, knowing no other way of life, struggled on as long as they could. The stubborness of a few men like Leslie Morton kept narrow-boat carrying afloat when it should really have sunk. It was still marginally convenient to carry coal from canal-side colliery to canal-side factory; goods like timber from over-side ship to canal-side timber yard. But industrial activity was no longer centred on canal banks and the mainstream of transport activity had long since left the canals as a series of backwaters.

Canal carrying had never been all beer and skittles, even in the Canal Age, with strong competition within the industry—and without, from coastal shipping, stage waggons and fly vans. Such problems were nothing to those which the railways brought from the 1840s. Still, even after the railways had become effectively competitive, canal carrying continued as a very substantial and important business. Tonnages carried on *some* canals did fall, but on many of the more important ones they were maintained and even increased down to 1898—twelve of the most important waterways increased their tonnage from about 13.6 million in 1848 to 18.4 million in 1898.

Many of these tons—often less valuable tons—were carried over much shorter distances than they had been before, at reduced rates, paying lower tolls, but many canals and carriers were surviving well enough, often, strange to say, under the benevolence of the railways. But much of the spirit had gone. There was little thought of innovation or expansion. They were second best and they knew it. This lack of confidence ill-prepared them for the next century.

Railways had stolen the glamour of movement and far-away places that had hung over canals and coaching (though more over the latter than the former). They poached many of the best men from both the older means of transport—agents, clerks, wharfingers and others, even boatmen, from the waterways. There was a labour force ready trained to be had by offering higher wages. Both Pennington and Baxendale, for example, deserted canals to become important railway men. In addition, boys venturing out upon a working life were more tempted by rapid locomotion, the art and mystery of the moving steam engine, than by the slow-moving life of the boats. Juvenile recruitment fell off. Regeneration on land as well as water became largely an hereditary process. Fewer recruits came from outside and some sons even disdained to follow their fathers. George Wilkes, for example, aged twenty-six in 1851, did not follow his parents onto the boats, but worked as a labourer on the railway at Stone.[2] 'Canal' fathers had 'railway' sons. In the 1850s and 1860s, and again from the 1890s, more men left the waterway industry than joined it.

It is ironic that it should have been the one and only great forward advance in canal engineering in Britain in the last 140 years which upset the rough equilibrium the canals had established in face of the railways. On 1 January 1894 the Manchester Ship Canal was opened and soon greatly emasculated the Liverpool–Manchester flat trade and with it many jobs. This was felt throughout the canal-boat industry. The surplus of boatmen kept wages down at a time of rising prices. Others joined the north-west boatmen leaving the waterways.[3]

This was simple enough. Many boatmen had always had permanent shore homes where their families lived. Being of the land as much as of the water it was not difficult for sons and even fathers to find work on land. Daughters who had been brought up on canals were being pushed out too—into domestic service—following the legislation of 1877 and 1884. Many did not return. Voyaging mothers were encouraged to live ashore permanently and some did, severing or straining their links, and those of their children, with waterway life.

Regeneration came increasingly from those families that had always lived permanently on board. Even these people were not the Flying Dutchmen that they have sometimes been made out to be, wandering endlessly from place to place to die aboard their boat. Some did. Some died before their time, but they were invariably transported back in their boat to be buried in some place that they called home even though they might never have lived on land there. Others retired with their savings and their memories—to Thrupp, Braunston, Buckby, Hawkesbury, Barnton, Winsford, Northwich, Thorne.

As we have seen quite a few watermen took up jobs like lock-keeping as age or infirmity made the work harder. They took up other trades too.

Mr E Shires, a boatman of long standing, for physical reasons has had to discontinue his employment on the canal boats. He is an excellent boot repairer and begs the patronage of the canal boat people with whom he has been associated all his life. He guarantees the best workmanship and leather at lowest reasonable charges. Boots may be left for him with the Leeds Lock-keeper and at the Riverside Mission.[4]

Charley Woodhouse retired to the family pub at North Kilworth in 1928 after working a pair of boats for the family coal business. David Hambridge's parents took over The Struggler at Banbury when they left the cut.

From the late nineteenth century men were increasingly leaving the waterways before their time. Men on all-male boats could make more on land. All boat people suffered from unemployment and underemployment in the 1920s and 1930s and many quit the life. Harry King had had enough by 1923. At the age of fifty-five he sold his boats to Samuel Barlow Canal Carriers of Tamworth and settled there. He finished his working life as a surface worker at Tamworth Colliery. He died at Tamworth in January 1945, two days after his wife, after fifty-six years together.

Emigration lured some boatmen away, especially in the 1920s when the Boatmen's Friend Society wrote how 'again during the year [1924] we have assisted numbers of our boys, who have grown tired of being workless, in their arrangements for securing passages to Australia and New Zealand'.

The lives of the canal people were influenced most of all by the two world wars. The first war took men out of the boats and from the banks and killed many of them. It was not so much their loss that affected boating as what the experiences of the war had done to those who came back. Nor was it at the front alone that they discovered more of the world on the other side of the towpath. Many, in both wars, went into munitions factories and other shore works, never to return to the waterways. 'New ideas, new attitudes, new horizons, new trades and occupations were revealed to them.'[5] In the second war, in addition to the problem of watermen being called up, the *Record* mentioned 'quite a number of men have left their employment and secured positions in the factories around the Birmingham district'. Many boatmen found temporary employment in factories during the hard winter frost of

Plates 35 and 36 The end: (*above*) narrow boats wait to unload their coal at Dickinson's paper mill, Watford, for the last time in 1967 (*Daily Telegraph*); (*below*) the Manchester Bolton & Bury Canal 1972 (*Author*)

1939–40. They discovered that they made more money there and stayed. The war brought added difficulties. Stop planks were put in on many canals at night to reduce the risk from bombing, but it also reduced the boatmen's earning potential. Rationing made it difficult for the shifting boat folk to get food. Jack Merrell, captain of the last Stoke Prior salt boat *Joan*, gave up when she was destroyed in a blitz on Birmingham in 1941. He took to salt-loading with no regrets.[6] David Hambridge sold his two boats to Barlows 'while the Germans were raiding Coventry and bosting open the canal'.[7] The dock area of London was a particularly discouraging place to be in on a canal boat in 1940 and 1941.

After World War II many boatmen were forced off the water-ways as carrier after carrier ceased to trade. Most merged into the industrial scene on land in factories in Coventry and Manchester, Birmingham and London. Men like John Hemelryk kept their connection with transport by driving lorries. Some of the Samuel Barlow boatmen transferred to driving the company's coal lorries or those of 'Jackson the Scrap' nearby.

Some left with great reluctance and maintained their connection with the waterways as long as they could. It was fortunate that the increase in pleasure cruising has meant that the canals must still be maintained. The waterways had an image of decadence and low wages so that limited recruitment into the land staff was leaving ever-older men to carry on the work. Not a few boatmen, in order to stay near the world they knew so well, got a job in canal maintenance. There were men like Fred Heritage—'I was born on the canal at Wolverhampton 31 years ago. My dad worked the Shroppy to Ellesmere Port for Fellows Morton and Clayton carrying all sorts of cargoes'. He was found dredging the Gower Arm in 1966.[8] In the same year, forty-one year old George Harris, who had spent a life time on the canals, had finished up as a tugman living in a British Waterway's cottage at Gas Street Basin, Birmingham. 'I can't stay away from canals,' he said. 'It breaks my heart to see old craft left to . . . sort of die, really. . . .'[9]

There had long been a tradition for watermen to take work as lock-keepers or in the easier canal land jobs as age wearied them of boating. Younger men were doing so as carrying was coming to an end. 'Jack' James ended his boating life by taking over the Stoke Bruerne locks in the 1940s where, in the 1960s, he twice won the Ritchie Rose Bowl for the country's best kept lock. In 1968 many of the lock-keepers on the Trent were former skippers. One Trent bargeman became a vicar.[10]

John Pennington started as a stable lad in Nottingham, becoming a horse driver and then, in 1924, mate on narrow boats and lighters. In 1958, by which time he was a captain, he left the water for the British Transport Waterway's Trent Lane depot where he had become assistant foreman by 1962.[11]

Some, like John Anderson, who had left the waterways completely, were always looking for ways to get back. He gave up his council house and a well paid job in a foundry in 1965 to join a new Midland carrying venture.

'I was born on a boat, the wife the same. When you've been brought up on the canal, you find you can't leave it all that easily.'[12] An earlier exile had wanted to return to the boats in 1952 because he found his house too draughty. Some 'permanent' boaters did find it difficult to adjust to living in a house as Eynsham Harry had forseen.

'I couldn't stop in a house look you,' he told Temple Thurston, 'I should catch cold the first night. 'Tis the same wi' any of us used to living on the boats. I haven't slept out of a boat since I was born.'

George Beechey, who had never slept under a roof or on dry land, was, in 1959, dreading the day when he must retire and live on shore.

Many boaters faced the prospect of an end to their waterway life with gloom. James Harrison, one of Willow Wren's steerers when the end of that company was foreshadowed in 1967, explained glumly that he had once worked in Coventry, but did not stay long. 'I could not settle away from the canals.'[13] Ken Nixon, one of the British Waterway's steerers just before the nationalized undertaking ceased trading in 1963, looked forward with apprehension to having to find a job ashore. 'Once it gets in your blood, you just can't get rid of it. It's such a free life.'[14]

We know about the feelings of these people because they clung to the canals to the bitter end, but there was a growing shortage of boatmen from the time of World War II. One would have expected a surplus as carriers went out of business. The truth was that as wages, working and living conditions improved on land, more and more boaters opted out of the continual grind in Spartan conditions (as in fact they had been doing in increasing numbers since the 1890s).

Wages were about £10–12 a week for the master of a pair of narrow boats in the early 1950s which, even after the labour value of a wife and son/hand were deducted, was a fair wage by the standards of the time and a relative improvement on pre-war rates.[15] But from then on wages stayed much the same. George Beechey was earning around £10 a week in 1959 to be shared with his wife and son.[16] John Hambridge could earn up to £16 for a week's work in the early 1960s working for British Transport Waterways, but he had to put in nearly eighty hours to get it.[17] James Harrison finished up with only around £10, after expenses, working a Willow Wren pair in 1967.[18] The wages of the men working wide boats—keels, flats and barges—kept up for longer, but the rapid advancement in living and working conditions of workers outside the canal industry made boating and canal work generally a less and less enviable way of life. Various training schemes, including the training of young women, were suggested and implemented, both during the war and after, but the shortage continued.

In short, many thousands of watermen left the hardships of the canals behind them with barely a backward glance; they soon became 'acclimatized' to their new life and merged into the general population. They might gaze wistfully over a canal bridge on occasion, reminisce now and again, but if asked to go back they would probably have said 'Never'.

Back in the eighteenth and early nineteenth centuries canals *had* provided a host of new opportunities of advancement for the working class. Even later in the century there was much to be said for canal life as compared with urban living. But time and technology were increasingly passing canals and canal people by, though many of them did not realize it because they knew no other way of life. If they found out it was a different story. Thomas Amos said in 1920, 'I am afraid the majority of them would not care to come back to boating again if they once got free from it'.[19] More and more of them did just that as the canals became increasingly a less eligible way of life.

A mist of nostalgic romanticism has crept over the waterways and their history. For some, canal life represented a survival of happier pre-industrial times. If we could but get back to that independent carefree life of yester-year all would be well. Visions are conjured up of the weaver at his hand loom; the potter at his wheel; the peasant upon his land, and especially the boatman on his boat, all happily surrounded by their families at work and play. But the cloth on the loom, the clay on the wheel, the long field of meadow to be mown with sickle or scythe, the canal boat to be unloaded of coal by hand must, at the thousandth viewing, have looked much like the thousandth Cortina at Dagenham or the millionth Mini at Longbridge. Perhaps there *was* more variety and freedom on the canals, but in the last century or so the boat people paid dearly for their independence and gradually they came to realize what sacrifices they were making.

Roses and castles have often been seen as encapsulating the freedom, beauty and culture of the simple peasant and artisan. Here was true fulfilment in artistic form and none were more fulfilled than the painters—the Herbert Tooleys and the Frank Nursers. But there was a thousandth rose too.

Frank Nurser painted boats at Braunston for the whole of his working life.

'How you must love painting,' Diane Doubtfire remarked as she examined the water can that she had bought from him.

'I could hardly believe my ears', she wrote later, still astonished, 'when he replied, "No, I hate painting!"'

Notes

All the canal company records (formerly British Transport Historical Records) are located at the Public Record Office (PRO), Kew, except where stated. Parliamentary papers (SCs, RCs, annual reports, etc), can be read in the House of Lords Record Office. HLRO indicates that they are available only there. The following abbreviations have been used in the notes:

    CRO = Cheshire County Record Office
     HC = House of Commons
     HL = House of Lords
    Lib = Reference Library
     RC = Royal Commission
     SC = Select Committee
    SRO = Staffordshire County Record Office
    WRO = Warwickshire County Record Office

NOTES TO CHAPTER I

1 Iredale, D. A. 'Canal Settlement . . . at Barnton . . . 1775-1845', unpublished PhD thesis, Leicester Univ (1966) 195
2 Register of Boats and Barges (Boat Register) (1795-1812) 156, CRO
3 Chambers, J. D., and Mingay, G. E. *The Agricultural Revolution* (1966); Bythell, D. *The Handloom Weavers* (1969)
4 Iredale, 1; Boat Register, 36
5 Poor Law Papers, PC 16/5/44, CRO; Boat Register, 292, WRO
6 Rideing, W. H. 'The Waterways of New York', *Harper's New Monthly Magazine*, Vol 48 (1873), 4
7 Malley, E. 'The financial administration of the Bridgewater estates, 1780–1800', unpublished MA thesis, Manchester Univ (1929), 21
8 *Aris* (1 June 1767)
9 Household, H. *The Thames and Severn Canal* (1969) 60
10 Malley. 21
11 Vine, P. A. L. *London's Lost Route to Basingstoke* (1968) 57
12 *Aris* (18 February 1793)
13 Vine, 45, quoting Shaw, S. *Tour of the West of England in 1788*

14 Broadbridge, S. R. *Birmingham Canal Navigations*, Vol 1 (1974) 17
15 *Aris* (1 June 1767)
16 *Maidstone Journal* (16 May 1820, 14 March 1822)
17 *Doncaster Gazette* (17 November 1815)
18 Rochdale Canal Minute Book (5 November 1795) Rochdale Canal Company
19 Manchester Bolton & Bury Canal Minute Book (26 August 1796)
20 Huddersfield Canal Minute Book (8 June 1797)
21 *Hull Advertiser* (10 March 1826), *Doncaster Gazette* (7 April 1815)
22 Hadfield, C. *British Canals* (1950; 1974) 41
23 Harris, H. *The Grand Western Canal* (1973) 38
24 Stevens, P. A. *The Leicester Line* (1972) 34
25 *Doncaster Gazette* (7 February 1817; 12 November 1841; 30 December 1842; 5 September 1823; 19 February, and 12 March 1830)

NOTES TO CHAPTER 2

1 *Standard* (4 September 1877) see also 6, 8 and 11 September
2 *Berrow's Worcester Journal* (26 July 1832)
3 *The Times* (27 August 1840)
4 *Staffordshire Advertiser* (12 October 1839)
5 *Doncaster Gazette* (19 June 1807)
6 'SC on Sunday Trading', *House of Lords Journal*, Vol 73, Appendix 2 (1841) 806
7 Pennington, Myles. *Railways and Other Ways* (1896) 28
8 Hollins, James. *Pastoral Recollections* (1857) 156
9 *The Waterman* (January 1898, February 1910)
10 Cubbon, T. W. *Only a little Cockboat* (1928) 22
11 *Waterman* (October 1928)
12 *Doncaster Gazette* (13 February 1835)
13 *Bromsgrove Messenger* (3 August 1962)
14 *Waterman* (March 1923)
15 Harlow, Alvin F. *Old Towpaths* (1926) 319, 329, 330
16 *The Record* (November 1923)
17 Northamptonshire RO, D3118
18 *Staffordshire Advertiser* (21 August 1840)
19 *Staffordshire Advertiser* (28 November 1840, 30 November 1839)
20 *Doncaster Gazette* (22 July 1831)
21 Birmingham Canal Company Letter Book (23 August 1814)
22 Northamptonshire RO, YZ 4026
23 Harlow, 318–19
24 *Aris* (22 November 1824)
25 *Standard* (4 September 1877)
26 Smith, George. *Canal Adventures by Moonlight* (1881) 84–5
27 *Staffordshire Advertiser* (16 May 1840)
28 *Bromsgrove Messenger* (3 August 1962)

1 *SC on Salt* (1818) 393, V, 339, pp 153–4; 164–5; *ibid.*, 300, p 12
2 Old Quay Order Book (1 October 1800; 3 August 1803; 4 September 1805; Bridgewater Department of Manchester Ship Canal Co
3 Colquhoun, Patrick. *A Treatise on the Commerce and Police of the River Thames* (1800) 246
4 *Doncaster Gazette* (15 January 1841)
5 *Staffordshire Advertiser* (27 June; 16 May 1840; 19 October 1839)
6 *Doncaster Gazette* (22 May 1840)
7 BBC Record 'Narrow Boats'
8 Pennington. 30
9 *The Times* (6, 7 August and 11 September 1823); *Morning Chronicle* (11 September 1823)
10 *SC on Railways* (1844) 318, xi, 44–51
11 Northamptonshire RO, GK 951 (1823)
12 *Staffordshire Advertiser* (22, 29 June, 27 July 1839; 21, 28 March, 11, 18 April 1840)

NOTES TO CHAPTER 4

1 *Annual Report of Ministry of Health, 1919–20*, 156
2 Iredale. 86
3 *Proceedings of Committee of Liverpool and Manchester Railroad Bill* (1825) 142; Boat Register, 106, CRO
4 Grand Junction Railway Bill (10 May 1838) 31, HLRO
5 *Harpers Monthly Magazine* (1885) 869
6 Calvert, Albert, F. *Salt in Cheshire* (1915) 435
7 Phillips, John. *A General History of Inland Navigation* (1805, 1970) 132
8 Hanson, Harry. *The Canal Boatmen, 1760–1914* (1975) 42
9 *Staffordshire Advertiser* (25 April 1840)
10 *Waterways*. British Waterways Board Magazine, (December 1965)
11 Birmingham Canal Journal (3 April 1773); Birmingham Canal Minute Books (1769–1776)
12 Market Weighton Canal Minute Book (22 July 1862) Market Weighton Drainage Board
13 Stevens. 98
14 Census (1871), RG 10 3722, 5, p 21, PRO
15 Shropshire Union [Railways and] Canal [Executive Committee] Minute Book (30 September 1885)
16 *Cooperative News* (15 January 1910)
17 Aire & Calder Navigation Minute Book (28 August 1817)
18 Iredale, 49, 89, 101, 245, Appendix 5, 99; Hanson, 57
19 Old Quay Order Book (7 September 1796); Malley, 159
20 *SC on Sunday Trading* (1841) 22, 954
21 Rideing. 11

22 *Doncaster Gazette* (14 February 1800, 31 August 1832)
23 Boat Register, 133, 127, CRO; 114, 117, 118, 106, WRO
24 Register of Vessels, City Archives, Hull; Old Quay Company (1 and 7 June 1814, 7 September 1796)

NOTES TO CHAPTER 5

1 *Doncaster Gazette* (31 December 1802, 21 March 1806)
2 Oxford Canal Company letters, Examination of Jas Stamps (25 May 1816)
3 Weaver Churches Bill [HC] (28 May 1840) 40–3, HLRO
4 Grand Junction Railway Bill [HC] (4 May 1838) 248, HLRO
5 *Monthly Labor Review* (February 1923), 227–8
6 1851 Census, HO 107, 2015, p 45; (1871) RG 10, 3089, 1, pp 26–7, PRO
7 *Bromsgrove Messenger* (3 August 1962)
8 Ministry of Health, *Report of the Departmental Committee Appointed to inquire into the practice of living-in on Canal Boats . . . (Committee on Living-in)* (1921) p6 and Min 1632
9 *Sunday Mercury* (23 July 1961)
10 *Committee on Living-in* (1921) mins, 1940, 519
11 *NSPCC Annual Report 1925-6*, 26
12 Fletcher, Harry. *A Life on the Humber: Keeling to Shipbuilding* (Faber & Faber, 1975) 60
13 Smith, George. *Our Canal Population* (1879) 11
14 Cubbon. 36, 45
15 *Committee on Living-in*, 394–5
16 *Doncaster Gazette* (30 June 1837)
17 Charles Hadfield Collection
18 *Nuneaton Chronicle* (8 April 1876)
19 *Standard* (8 September 1877)
20 1871 Census, RG 10, 3883, 6, p 4; (1861) RG 9, 1926, p 139
21 *Annual Report of Ministry of Health for 1925-6*, 180
22 *Northwich Chronicle* (14 December 1935, 11 January 1936)
23 *Cooperative News* (15 January 1910)
24 1871 Census, RG 10, 3722, 5, p 37
25 Smith. *Canal Adventures*, 76–8
26 Weaver Navigation Minute Book (5 February 1789; 4 September 1788; 5 August 1801; 3 March 1803) CRO
27 Stourbridge Canal Minute Book (3 June 1830)
28 Monmouthshire Canal Minute Book (3 April 1837)
29 Derby Canal Minute Book (15 February 1866, 22 December 1869) Derbyshire RO
30 Fletcher. 31
31 Grand Union Canal Minute Book (12 November 1817)
32 Northamptonshire RO, D2115
33 Weaver Navigation Minute Book (6 March; 1 May 1843; 1 February 1847) CRO

NOTES TO CHAPTER 6

1 Townshend, Thomas. *A Plan for the Amalgamation of Canals between London and Liverpool* (1846) 4, 24
2 'Hercules'. *British Railways and Canals* (c 1885) 94
3 *The Times* (15 August 1921)
4 Stevens. 147
5 *The Times* (15 August 1921)
6 Harlow. 335
7 *Standard* (8 September 1877)
8 *SC on Canals* (1883) 505; *SC on Canal Boats* (1884), 489, 1148–9
9 Ringwalt, J. L. *Development of the Transportation System in the United States* (1888) 54
10 *SC on Canal Boats* (1884) 1152–3
11 Harlow. 334
12 *Warrington Examiner* (23 December 1876)
13 Shropshire Union Canal Minute Book (25 February 1914)
14 *SC on Canal Boats* (1884) 1272–3
15 Birmingham Canal Minute Book (29 July; 8 November 1776; 12 August 1774)
16 Brecon & Abergavenny Canal Minute Book (11 December 1813)
17 Erewash Canal Minute Book (2 May 1815)
18 Weaver Churches Bill [HC] (1 June 1840) 84, (29 May 1840) 54, HLRO
19 *Liverpool and Manchester Railroad Bill* (1825) 14, 145, 147

NOTES TO CHAPTER 7

1 *Manchester Guardian* (30 October 1825)
2 *Doncaster Gazette* (1 January 1808)
3 Grand Junction Railway Bill [HC] (10 May 1838) 60, HLRO
4 *Doncaster Gazette* (13 May 1825)
5 *Sunday Mercury* (30 December 1973)
6 *Aris* (14 November 1803)
7 *NSPCC Annual Report, 1928–9*, 26; *Yorkshire Gazette* (3 May 1794, 13 September 1794); *Doncaster Gazette* (14 July 1826); Shropshire Union Canal Minute Book (14 October 1908)
8 *Child's Guardian* (August 1920, August 1921)
9 *Hull Advertiser* (15 September 1826)
10 *Doncaster Gazette* (25 July 1802); Shropshire Union Canal Minute Book (19 June 1901)
11 *Doncaster Gazette* (28 July 1833)
12 *Sunday Mercury* (9 October 1966)
13 *Aris* (11 January 1802)
14 *Navigation* (May 1969)
15 *Rugby Advertiser* (21 January 1854)
16 *Sunday Mercury* (9 October 1966)

217

17 Birmingham Canal Minute Book (30 June 1775; 9 October 1778; 13 April 1770)
18 *Waterman* (September 1896)
19 *Doncaster Gazette* (11 July 1834)
20 Norton, Peter in *Journal of the Railway and Canal Historical Society* (November 1976)
21 *Derby Mercury* (21 April 1803)
22 Oxford Canal Company, in-letters (February 1817)
23 *The Times* (3 March 1824)
24 Harlow. 316–8
25 *Record* (May 1949) 287
26 *Standard* (8 September 1877)
27 *Manchester Guardian* (28 January 1925)
28 *Local Government Board (LGB) Report for 1889–90*, 220; *1887*, 121; *1885*, 69
29 Lambert, R. F. in *The Daily Telegraph* (15 August 1962)
30 *Manchester Guardian* (14 September 1923)

NOTES TO CHAPTER 8

1 Information drawn from NSPCC annual reports for 1920s unless indicated otherwise
2 *Runcorn Examiner* (14 April 1877)
3 *Record* (December 1921)
4 Parr, Robert J. *Canal Boat Children* (1910) 27–8
5 *Child's Guardian* (November 1927)
6 Shropshire Union Canal Minute Book (14 February 1900)
7 *Monthly Labor Review* (February 1923) 235–6
8 Lambert, R. F. in *The Daily Telegraph* (15 August 1962)
9 Parr. 13
10 *Monthly Labor Review* (February 1923) 246
11 *SC on Sunday Trading* (1841) 954
12 Harlow. 328
13 King, E. J. in *Waterways* (April 1959)
14 *Child's Guardian* (November 1910)
15 Cubbon. 56
16 Parr. 11
17 *Child's Guardian* (February 1919)
18 *Standard* (4 September 1877)
19 *Monthly Labor Review* (1923)
20 *Record* (February, August 1927; June 1929)
21 *Annual Report of the Ministry of Health, 1923–4*, 147
22 Elliott, William J. (Ed), *Children on Canal Boats* (1929) 8; Bird, V. in *Birmingham Weekly Post* (18 April 1952)
23 *LGB Report for 1905*, 82–3
24 *Hansard* (9 May 1930) 1369–70

25 *Ibid* (31 January 1930) 1387, 1440
26 *Record* (May 1930)
27 Rolt, L. T. C. *Inland Waterways of England* (1950; 1970) 158, 178

NOTES TO CHAPTER 9

1 *SC on Sunday Trading* (1841) 750
2 *Hansard* (31 January 1930) 1398, 1390
3 *Aris* (31 October 1825)
4 *Quarterly Review* (1843–4) 281–324; Malley; Sutcliffe, John. *A Treatise on Canals and Reservoirs* (1816) 128; Malet, Hugh. *The Canal Duke* (1961)
5 Old Quay Order Book (4 July 1837, 4 December 1837); *SC on Sunday Trading* (1841) 795, 824–7, 806
6 Diary of G. R. Bird (1820–30) Birmingham Lib
7 *Transport Saga, 1646–1947: the History of Pickfords* (1947) 17
8 Lea, George. *Memoir of the Reverend John Davies . . .* (1860) 173
9 *Household Words* (18 September 1858) 321
10 *LGB Report for 1889–90*, 224
11 *The Daily Telegraph* (27 June 1925)
12 *Committee on Living-in* (1921) 1730
13 Saxon, John in *Waterways World* (September 1976)
14 *Record* (May 1930)
15 *SC on Sunday Trading* (1841) 532, 741
16 *Ibid*, 706–12; Malet, 174–5
17 *SC on Sunday Trading* (1841) 741
18 Cubbon. 46–7
19 *Committee on Living-in* (1921) 857, 1907
20 *Ibid*, 419
21 *NSPCC Report, 1928–9*, 27; *1921–2*, 13
22 *Record* (April 1923)

NOTES TO CHAPTER 10

1 *Manchester Guardian* (14 September 1923)
2 *Record* (September–December 1923; May, June 1927)
3 *Waterman* (April 1924)
4 Hanson. 69
5 Old Quay Order Book (15 August 1796)
6 Shropshire Union Canal Minute Book (16 February 1910, 18 October 1911); Hanson, 96–7
7 *Canal Journal* (October 1892); *Liverpool Review* (27 August, 10 September 1892)
8 *Aris* (31 January 1774)
9 *Record* (March 1938); *Child's Guardian* (November 1910)
10 *Doncaster Gazette* (8 February 1822)

11 *Waterman* (March, October 1894, June 1898)
12 *Ibid* (February 1894); *LGB Report for 1899–1900*, 194
13 *Committee on Living-in* (1921) 222, 220
14 *RC on Labour (Group B), Transport and Agriculture*, Vol III, 1893–4, 17104
15 *Record* (August 1929); *Statistical Abstract of the U.K., 1922–35* (1936–7) [Cmd 5353] xxvi, 137
16 See *The Record*, especially August 1931, November 1935, June and August 1938, June 1943, January 1947
17 *Waterman* (December 1929)
18 *NSPCC Report, 1926–7*, 27

NOTES TO CHAPTER 11

1 Information on the Kings is drawn from: *Diary of W. H. King—Canal Contractor* (1895) at the British Waterways Museum; Registers of Canal Boats (1879—) Paddington Town Hall; Trevor King; *Waterways* (April 1959)
2 Hanson. 111, 104–7
3 *LGB Report for 1895*, 240
4 Boat Register (1795) 126–7; Will of Thomas Haslehurst, WS (2 June 1798) CRO
5 Will of John Hind (October 1821) Lancashire RO
6 Waterways Museum
7 *RC on Canals*, Vol 1 (1906) 4431, 4436
8 Boat Register (1795) 175–179, 92, 45, 164, CRO
9 Will of John Ashton, WS (March 1773) CRO
10 Boat Register (1795) 66; Will of Robert Poole, WS (3 February 1810); Robert Denton, WS (4 June 1836) CRO
11 *Doncaster Gazette* (8 December 1843)
12 *Monthly Labor Review* (1923)
13 Birmingham Canal Bill [HC] (21 April 1839) 164–205, HLRO
14 Canal Scrapbook compiled by Reginald Wood, Rochdale Lib
15 *Committee on Living-in* (1921) 1200–3

NOTES TO CHAPTER 12

1 *Coventry Evening Telegraph* (17 July 1968)
2 *The Daily Telegraph* (27 June 1925)
3 *Waterman* (December 1922)
4 MH 32/94, 'Draft Report for 1889', 39000/90, PRO
5 Gilian Statham in *Warwickshire and Worcestershire Magazine*, late 1950s
6 *Waterman* (May 1897)
7 Lambert, R. F. in *The Daily Telegraph* (15 August 1962)
8 *Committee on Living-in* (1921) 76
9 Wilkinson, Tim. *Hold on a Minute* (1965) 129
10 *SC on Sunday Trading* (1841) 615

11 *Liverpool and Manchester Railroad Bill* (1825) 605
12 *SC on the Laws Relating to the Salt Duty* (1818) 383, V, 88, 157, 190, 193, 153
13 Hodder, Edwin. *George Smith [of Coalville]: The Story of an Enthusiast* (1896) 71
14 Cubbon. 181–2
15 *Daily Mail* (3 December 1959)
16 *Waterways* (early 1960s)
17 *Warwickshire Journal* (date unknown)
18 Hodder. 72
19 Harlow. 330
20 Hodder. 72
21 Temple Thurston, E. *The Flower of Gloster* (1911) 69
22 Aubertin, C. J. *A Caravan Afloat* (1916) 100
23 *Manchester Evening News* (20 March 1919)
24 *Annual Report of Ministry of Health, 1930–1*, 273–4

NOTES TO CHAPTER 13

1 *Sunday Mercury* (23 July 1961)
2 Census (1851) HO 107, 2,000, 368–1, 162
3 Based on research by Mary Prior.
4 *Waterman* (November 1926)
5 Parker, Rowland. *The Common Stream* (1975)
6 *Bromsgrove Messenger* (3 August 1962)
7 *Sunday Mercury* (23 July 1961)
8 *Ibid* (9 October 1966)
9 *Birmingham Post* (27 August 1966)
10 Pettitt, Rev R. in *Navigation* (early 1968)
11 *Waterways* (December 1962)
12 *Motor Boat and Yachting* (5 November 1965)
13 *The Daily Telegraph* (14 January 1967)
14 *TV Times* (8 April early 1960s)
15 Bird, V. in *Birmingham Weekly Post* (18 April 1952); material loaned by David Campbell
16 *Daily Mail* (3 December 1959)
17 Lambert, R. F. 'Education v the Canal' in unidentified newspaper
18 *The Daily Telegraph* (14 January 1967)
19 *Committee on Living-in* (1921) 1138

Index